Dear Dr. Wes…

Real Life Advice for Teens

Wes Crenshaw, PhD

With Teen Co-authors

Jenny Kane, Marissa Ballard Hemenway, John Murray,
Julia Davidson, Kelly Kelin Woods, Samantha Schwartz,
Ben Markley, and Miranda Davis

Based on the
Double Take Column
In the Lawrence Journal World

Publisher's Cataloging-in-Publication
(Provided by Quality Books, Inc.)

Crenshaw, Wes.
    Dear Dr. Wes : real life advice for teens / Wes
Crenshaw ; with teen co-authors Jenny Kane ... [et al.].
    p. cm.
    Based on the Double take column in the Lawrence
journal world.
    LCCN 2011944954
    ISBN-13: 978-0615570419
    ISBN-10: 0615570410

    1. Teenagers--Conduct of life--Juvenile literature.
[1. Teenagers--Conduct of life.]   I. Kane, Jenny.
II. Title. III. Title: Lawrence journal-world.

BJ1661.C74 2011   158.1
               QBI11-600226

Published in the United States of America by

FAMILY PSYCHOLOGICAL PRESS
www.familypsychpress.com

Also available on Kindle from Amazon.com

PRAISE FOR DEAR DR. WES...REAL LIFE
ADVICE FOR TEENS

"I LOVE these books! The advice offered by Wes and his co-authors is right on, straightforward and down to earth; an extremely relevant and thoughtful synthesis of a professional reference work and Dear Abby. I say this in a most complimentary way, as I've never experienced any work more effective and relevant in responding to today's unique teen and parent issues. Wes Crenshaw's years of professional experience provide, in combination with the input of eight responsible teen co-authors, a wealth of wisdom. I completely recommend these books as a "must-read" for teens and their parents."

—**Foster W. Cline, M.D.**, bestselling author of the *Parenting with Love and Logic* materials, and co-founder with Jim Fay of the Love and Logic Institute.

"These invaluable books offer the true depth of color of the contemporary teen experience which other works merely outline. Parents and their teenagers should not attempt the journey through adolescence without the wonderful wisdom in these pages."

—**Michael Bradley, Ed.D.**, bestselling author of *When Things Get Crazy With Your Teen: The Why, the How, and What to DO NOW.*

"If you want good realistic, useful advice for parents and teens, Dear Dr. Wes: Real Advice for Teens and Parents is a great read. It's a wonderful example of how advice for teens and their parents should be presented; as a true collaboration between a mental health professional and young people. I recommend both books highly!"

— **Rosalind Wiseman**, bestselling author of *Queen Bees and Wannabes*, internationally recognized expert on teen girls, relational aggression, social justice, and ethical leadership.

This is a great resource for parents. Buy it now and start reading—so that you'll have some ideas ready before problems hit. It would also make a fine gift for parents and kids on the cusp of teenageism. Imagine if they read the questions and discussed the answers together. Even if they didn't agree, (1) they'd be talking, and (2) they would be exchanging ideas and clarifying values about what is good and bad, right and wrong, healthy and not. It would be a Triple Take—Dr. Wes, his teenage column associates, and the readers! I recommend it wholeheartedly!

> —**Michael Hoyt, PhD**, author of *Some Stories are Better than Others, The Present is a Gift, and Brief Psychotherapies;* and editor of *Therapist Stories of Inspiration, Passion and Renewal: What's Love Got to Do with it?;* and parent of a 24-year-old son.

I loved these two books—real questions from real people. One is for parents, needing answers as they navigate the rough waters of adolescence. The other for teens - those incredible, brilliant, energetic, maddening creatures leaping (often without looking) into adulthood, one foot lagging behind in childhood. The answers provided by Wes and the teen writers are always compassionate, always on everyone's side—thoughtful, blunt and sometimes raw in their honesty. These books should sit side by side on the shelf. Yes, there's one for parents and one for teens, but read BOTH! If you're a teen, you might see where your parents are coming from and how much they care. If you're a parent, you'll remember what you were like at fifteen, and more importantly, glimpse how challenging, how really challenging, it is these days to grow up healthy and happy.

> — **Linda Daugherty** received the 2011 National Award from the Society for Adolescent Health and Medicine for her plays dealing with teen issues, *The Secret Life of Girls, Eat (It's Not About Food), dont u luv me?* and *hard 2 spel dad* (written with Mary Rohde Scudday). She has also been nominated by the Dallas Morning News arts staff for 2011 Dallas Morning News Texan of the Year. Her plays have been produced worldwide. She is playwright in residence at Dallas Children's Theater, named by Time Magazine as one of the top five theaters in the U.S. for families and youth, and a member of the Dramatists Guild of America.

DEDICATION

*To our readers who've
kept Double Take in the paper
and online every week since 2004.*

CONTENTS

Contents

All opinions and advice expressed herein belong solely to the authors and are not intended to substitute for psychological services. Readers are encouraged to seek professional guidance as necessary.

Email your questions about life as a teen to:

Ask@dr-wes.com

ACKNOWLEDGMENTS

Many thanks to the staff of the Family Therapy Institute Midwest for sponsoring the Double Take student scholarship from 2007 to 2010; and to Central National Bank for its additional funding. We owe a huge debt of gratitude to the Lawrence Journal World for giving ink to the only newspaper column on the planet that offers teenagers the chance to write advice to their parents and peers and for tolerating the controversies we sometimes create in the process.

Thanks also to Christine DeSmet, Faculty Associate at the University of Wisconsin-Madison for her ongoing consultation on the art and business of writing; Barrett Swanson, MFA for his keen editing and attention to the details of the English language; and the Kansas City Writers Group and e-Publishing Group for their support and encouragement of this project.

A final word of thanks to my mom, Marilyn Crenshaw, who finally got a chance to put her high school English award to the test as a proofreader; and to my daughter, Alyssa for her excruciatingly detailed read of the proofs.

ACKNOWLEDMENTS

How true Daddy's words were when he said: all children must look after their own upbringing. Parents can only give good advice or put them on the right paths, but the final forming of a person's character lies in their own hands.

Anne Frank,
Diary of A Young Girl

1 DOUBLE TAKE

Good advice for teenagers. Everyone has some, or thinks they do. Friends, family, the Internet. The problem is that for advice to be really good, it must be equal parts empathy and wisdom. To make sense of your world, the giver must feel things the way you feel them and see things the way you see them, before offering up an opinion.

"Clean your room," "You have to go to college," or "Don't have sex 'til you're married" sound like good advice. Or, maybe someone is just trying to persuade you to think the way they do. At this age, you're more interested in finding your own way of thinking. So, rather than just marketing one person's version of reality, good advice instead challenges you to see as many sides of a problem as possible before making a decision.

"Bad advice" is usually easier to spot and harder to ignore. "Smoke this, it's great" probably isn't the best suggestion you'll get this Saturday night. But how many of your friends fall in line whenever they hear it? How about, "Don't worry, you won't get pregnant if [we only do it once/I pull out/you're on your period]?" That's about as phony as it sounds, yet this kind of bad advice keeps showing up at the most inconvenient moments.

Bad advice never challenges you to think. It just asks you to obey.

You have to be smart about where you get your advice, because everyone has an angle. Some of those angles are legit. Your parents have a major investment in your going to college and delaying pregnancy. So, try and forgive them if they seem to push those ideas pretty hard. They may even fear that an unclean room will lead you to a life of filthy apartments and lost marriages. Who knows? It could happen.

Other angles are ridiculous. Your friends may put great stock in getting you crazy drunk, or some random boy may really "need" to hook up with you, or your teacher may beg you to join everything because you're such a go-getter. An overly anxious parent might hover, constantly criticizing and nitpicking, while advising that you'll never change. A coach or Sunday School teacher might ask you to do something sexually inappropriate. So, dealing with advice, regardless of its source, means examining those angles and understanding who's pushing them.

Good advice is always benevolent—meaning it's given with your best interests in mind, even if it pisses you off at the time. In fact, a lot of good advice will do just that, and a lot of bad advice will feel pretty good at the time you're taking it.

I was reminded yet again of just how smart teenagers are and how smart you have to be to get through this big, complex world we've left for you.

The advice in this book is unusual because the folks pushing it aren't hip middle-aged experts talking to you in what they imagine to be cool teen voices that they vaguely remember from 1977. Well, okay…one of us is. I'm a board certified family psychologist.[1] But the other eight co-authors are really sharp teenagers, or were at the time they wrote for Double Take, a weekly advice column that has been published in the Lawrence Journal World since 2004. Seven were high school seniors and one was an exceptional junior. Each won a contest to work for a year on Double Take. Most of these columns were written in response to letters, many submitted by teenagers. The rest discussed topics we selected from current events and trends affecting teens.

Double Take and this book are frank, honest, and sometimes blunt. We discuss sex, contraception, pregnancy, sexual identity, cutting, falling in love, breaking up, finding new friends and treating the ones you have ethically, divorce, marriage, college, suicide, foster care, school, fear and hope, and a bunch of other issues you get up and face every morning. I know this because I've faced them too, over nineteen years and thousands of hours working with teens.

---

[1] I'm a licensed psychologist and Board Certified in Couples and Family Psychology by the American Board of Professional Psychology.

I hope you and your parents have the kind of relationship where you can go to them with all your concerns on these topics. In fact, in our other book,[2] we bug your folks to start these kinds of conversations when you're about five and to continue having them until you're in your mid-twenties. But if they didn't get the memo in time, or if you just don't feel comfortable discussing how to handle your love life, drunken friends, sexual orientation, fears about the future, or frustration with school, read this book. Then, have your parents read our other book. Then, exchange books. While we want to offer you and your parents wise, empathic guidance, we really want to encourage each of you to have more empathy and wisdom for one another.

You can read this book cover-to-cover and take careful notes if you want, then pass it on to your friends. Better yet, buy them a copy. I have a teenage girl of my own, and some of the co-authors are still in college or just starting careers, so we need the money! ☺

You can also use this as a reference book. We've set up the chapters and column titles to help you find what you need when dealing with your most recent *crisis de jour*. Either way you use it, by the time you're out of your freshman year of college, I bet you'll have found your way through just about every topic in this book, and most of those in the other book, too. If we've missed something, email us and we'll answer your question in the column.

As I was doing final edits on this book, I still found myself laughing on one page and near tears on the next. But, more than anything, I was reminded yet again of just how smart teenagers are and how smart you have to be to get through this big, complex world we've left for you.

Hopefully, Double Take will be around in twenty years so you can buy the updated version for your kids. I can't imagine what we'll be talking about then. Probably how much time your teen should be allowed to spend each day accessing the video chip in his head, or something.

That's what's fun about this job. You never know what's coming.

So here's my first piece of hip, wise, empathic advice: *As you cross the bridge to adulthood, never forget that your ultimate goal is to become who you are.*

We hope the advice in this book will help.

—Wes Crenshaw, PhD ABPP
ask@dr-wes.com

---

2 *Dear Dr. Wes…Real Life Advice for Parents of Teens.*

2 LOVE

Snow Day Couple

Dr. Wes: The young couple warmed the whole restaurant on a cold afternoon. Their principal had called a snow day and they knew exactly how to spend it—together.

I couldn't take my eyes off them. Frequent readers of Double Take know my guilty pleasures. I love watching the antics of playfully close families, or witnessing couples lost in each other's company. For this couple at Chili's, the whole world had disappeared, leaving only the space around them. They never noticed me across the room with my "aw, how cute" smile.

She hadn't worn makeup that day. She didn't need to. She adorned the booth, wearing an old white T-shirt and sweats, safe and comfortable. On some unspoken cue, she leaned across the table and shared a kiss, sweet and perfect, with her boy. She talked and laughed, entertaining him. No texting or video games or DVDs or Internet needed. He never took his eyes from her, noticing her every detail. He grabbed her hands across the table. She lit up again.

Love is more than attraction and lust. It takes effort and work.

"I wonder how long they've been together," I said to my kids. "It looks like a week or a month maybe. They've so much to say and—"

"No, Daddy," my thirteen-year-old daughter said. "You're not going to talk to them."

"How about you?" I asked my kindergarten son. "Men with cute little boys can talk to anyone. You'd go over there with me, wouldn't you?"

"I'm going to the car," he said.

They hid in the entryway, like they were waiting for the bus.

I can't help it. It's my respite from the office, where I see couples of all ages creating disasters for each other. Forgetting what it felt like to be lost in that space with their partners, sometimes imagining they could go back there, if they just found someone else. Always wanting to be where they're not.

Neither the boy nor girl was surprised when I told them they were the cutest couple in the history of the world. Not a bit. They just giggled, as if they got that all the time. Anyone who loves love would see it and want to celebrate it with them. She's sixteen. He's seventeen. They've been together for an entire year and still give off the energy of the day they met. It's like their first date again, today in that booth.

We can debate the wisdom of such intense love at this age. We've done it before in this column. But whomever that boy and girl end up marrying, I can tell you this: each will know how to love their partners, to entertain them, to notice them, and make a space just for them. That's what they're practicing now.

Dear teens whose parents have dropped this column by the breakfast plate on this manic Tuesday morning, I have just one wish for you: Feel that.

Toss everything you know about hooking up and hanging out. Just trash it. Don't cling desperately to a guy or girl who treats you like crap. Go on strike until someone looks at you like that couple looked at each other, warming the room with love for one another. A hundred hookups from now, you'll never find what that young couple finds every day across the table, together, effortlessly.

You can blow it off. Say they're one in a million. Not normal. But I've seen hundreds of couples, young and old who know how to love like that. Nothing is stopping you from becoming one of them.

Trust me on this one.

Samantha Schwartz: What struck me about Wes's story was the amount of time the couple has been together. Not just two weeks or a few months. A year.

Almost any couple can make it a month or two and still look like that. Everything is just so easy in that lovey-dovey, get-to-know-ya period. You have yet to discover the other person's flaws, and their weird habits still seem "charming." Getting past the honeymoon and into real life is a difficult transition, but the strongest couples have made it there together.

Any fans of *The Bachelor* out there? Last Monday, Jake proposed to Vienna, the girl with whom he had less of an emotional connection and more of a physical one. Vienna told Jake that she wanted her marriage to be "Just like being teenagers in love every day." Yeah, okay.

Love is more than attraction and lust. It takes effort and work.

I doubt Wes's restaurant couple are close by accident. They probably worked at it. After a year of dating, they're bound to have had conflicts, and they must have talked them out. They've made each other a priority. Decided to spend the snow day together, even though they could have used it in a hundred other ways. They built trust so they could tear down the barricades we all put up to protect our hearts. And Wes is right, that's what love is about.

Maybe they'll write in and tell us how they did it.

Ben's Relationship Clinic

Ben Markley: What if there was a health clinic for relationships? If you could just walk in for a checkup, what would the doctor say? Until that clinic gets some funding, here are a few diagnoses I've seen in both couples and friendships. You might check your relationships to see whether any of these apply.

Addiction. One person cannot become your one-and-all. It's great to care deeply for someone, but you cannot put all your chips on one person, especially in pre-graduation years. If your social life rests on the shoulders of a single person, then you're looking at a painful bout of "rehab" if he or she ever leaves.

Cancer. We always hurt the ones we love, but we sometimes make someone's bad choice synonymous with his or her identity. Are there any people whom you identify by what they did to you, rather than by who they are? If you let that resentment fester, the cancer will spread to every aspect of your relationship until it's deceased. The only cure is for both parties to confront it, stat.

Heart problems. If you can't be real with the person you're dating or if they don't like the person you are (i.e. they're always trying to change you), then your relationship probably isn't going anywhere too great. If you can't accept an unabridged version of each other, then that's going to play out poorly down the road.

Brain damage. Think about it. Do you have friends that consistently do things you know are wrong? Do they drag you down with them? If so, cut out the tumor before the damage gets worse.

Hallucinations. You're not dating the perfect person (because they don't exist), so don't pretend that you are. You put a lot of pressure on someone when you idealize them, and it's going to hurt both of you when they inevitably shatter your illusion.

Hypochondria. When one joke or criticism sends your significant other into a state of panic, you've probably got dating hypochondria. A hypochondriac always assumes something is wrong with your relationship. We all experience this sort of anxiety to an extent, but we have to be careful that it doesn't mess with our heads. Insecurity often leads to doubt, and nothing poisons a relationship like a lack of trust.

Any of these sound familiar? If so, don't just slap a Band-Aid on your problem and call it resolved. Whether you need to have a sincere talk with someone or you need to break up, most of these problems require surgery.

Take the time. Don't ignore the symptoms.

Dr. Wes: Lucky us! Such clinics do exist. Most therapists know that mental health conditions are often related to social and relationship environments. So, based on many years working that way, I'll extend a couple of Ben's points.

Trying to reengineer someone into whom you think they should be usually ends badly, no matter how positive the changes you envision. That said, most serious friendships and any good romance will change both partners. That's one of the attractions in getting close to

Even if there's no perfect someone waiting for you, there are a great many someones who you might be perfect with.

anyone. Your job in choosing a partner is to determine whether a given individual's core personality can stand the upgrade and whether he or she really wants to be different.

Simply put, most people want to change, but not very much.

The next most common relationship mistake is expecting too little. There are no flawless people, but there are quite a few who don't self-destruct at every turn and take their partners with them. Many are good-hearted, have goals and ambitions, aren't drunk or high much of the time, and disavow abusive or antisocial behavior. If you see any of those problems creeping into your relationship, push the eject button.

Trying to change such folks usually enables more of the same.

Even if there's no perfect someone waiting for you, there are a great many someones who you might be perfect with—if you give yourself a chance to sort them out.

The third most common mistake I see is settling for a poorly matched partner simply because you don't believe you can "trade up." Instead, get up every day and assume you deserve the best relationship you can find. Then, go looking for it.

Here's a few more of my little rules for that search:

- Always look for someone who is better than you, then let them lift you up, gently.
- Never be with anyone you have to be with, lest you become powerless in the relationship. All relationships are paradoxical that way.
- The neediest party in a couple is the most motivated to be in the relationship and the most motivated person is always the one with the least power. If you find yourself in a severely power-mismatched relationship, the best thing you can do is get out or at least make the other party aware that you could do so. There is no other way to level the playing field.

We like to think of relationships as feeling-based. That's fine when you're trying to get one going, but things tend to come out better when you really think them through. Give your relationship a little courageous thought and see what you find.

Shopping for Boys

Dear Dr. Wes and Marissa,

I've been hanging out with a guy for about two months now. We go on long walks and spend hours just talking and debating politics, philosophy, etc. It feels as if we've known each other for all our lives. The drawback is that he has a girlfriend he's been dating for three years who lives fifty miles away. He always complains about her. The other night we got in an argument and I said he was leading me on and we shouldn't talk anymore; he said he likes me but doesn't have the courage to tell his girlfriend. Today he gave me a CD of a musical I love and now it's making me doubt my decision. I don't know what to do anymore. I really like this guy and I see myself with him, but I cannot be treated like this and I know I can't just continue to be his friend. What should I do?

Dr. Wes: Love is like shopping for a good pair of jeans. You generally get what you pay for in quality, style, and substance. However, when you don't make the right selection, jeans rarely hurt as much as love does. On this shopping spree, you're headed for a world of hurt.

We can tell right off the bat that this guy has some quality problems because he's essentially cheating on his girlfriend with you. Perhaps you haven't gone far physically, but he's certainly being untrue to her by hanging out with you and sharing his complaints about her. For married couples, we call this an "emotional affair" and it can be more hurtful than a physical one.

From your perspective, the most seductive aspect of the situation is that you believe you will be the one person that he can truly love, that you will be good enough to turn his head and make him true to you. Just remember, that's what the current girlfriend thought at some point, especially if they've been dating for three years. It's easy to see her as a kind of enemy because she's standing between you and Mr. Right. He takes advantage of that by assuming the victim role, badmouthing her and making you his special confidant.

Of course, anyone may meet their perfect match while dating someone else. Your guy is pretty young to be making a three-year commitment, so I could understand if he wanted to break up with her to be with you. But that *isn't* what he's doing and your instincts were right not to stand for it. He needs to be in one relationship at a time, and if he isn't, then he's playing both of you.

If he really is the one perfect guy for you, this is no way to start a relationship. He should come back when he's grown up a bit and made some decisions about how to behave with integrity.

Marissa Ballard[3]: Perhaps more serious than finding a good pair of jeans, finding love is especially difficult. The good news comes first: You have plenty of time. Now, the bad news: You still haven't found it. Even though he sounds good in theory, there's one blazing red flag that should have you running in the other direction: The girlfriend. Let's take a minute to examine the situation objectively.

Picture yourself with a friend in your situation. Here she is, becoming attached to this seemingly charming, wonderful young man who says he likes and wants to be with her, but he won't end a relationship with a girl an hour away to do it. Don't you see yourself getting a bad vibe? Fifty miles away is not a long drive. Relationships have survived ten times that distance and badmouthing her shows a lack of respect for women. At the very least, it's tacky. That won't change just because he's with you.

I am glad you stood up for yourself and I hope you continue to do so. The CD was a peace offering and it would be unwise to keep it. Leave this guy to figure out what he wants. You're not doing yourself any favors by giving him the chance to hurt you. Sure, it's fun to discuss politics and philosophy with a nice piece of eye candy, but that's all there is to this.

Find some candy that isn't already purchased.

Bad Boys and Nice Girls

Dear Dr. Wes and Jenny,

Why are nice girls so attracted to bad boys?

Dr. Wes: You didn't tell us if you are a guy or girl and I think the implications are different for each. If you're the nice girl or her mom, you may be lamenting previous dating choices. If you're a nice guy, you probably feel you don't get an even break in the dating world.

I work with a lot of teenage girls and young women. In fact, they form the majority of my caseload. Yet, even I remain puzzled by this question. It just seems so contrary that a nice, respectable girl would find herself linking arms with the "bad boys," rather than all those guys

---

[3] Marissa Ballard married in July 2010, four years after completing her tenure on Double Take. Her column bylines remain under her unmarried name, though she is listed as Marissa Hemenway for the authorship of this book.

who've committed themselves to the journey to sainthood. So, I took this opportunity to interview a panel of teenage girl experts, all of whom told me that I was overthinking this issue. One said that dating nice boys is too much like dating her brother. Or, as another put the equation, "Bad boys equal adrenaline rush."

Others noted that nice girls tend to have less than exciting lives because. One said, "If we're honest, being a nice girl means that you follow all of the rules. 'Bad' boys are more inclined to act in ways that are unfamiliar—and therefore exciting—to nice girls. They stretch our limits and introduce us to new things." That's enough to scare most of their parents, I'm sure, but for nice girls, it seems to strike the right chord.

So what's a nice guy to do? First, I suggest not trying to "go bad" just to snare all those nice girls. At no time is a poser easier to spot than when a nice boy decides to run with the wolves. More importantly, bad boys are only winners until everyone gets older, when girls begin making real choices about which guys they want to spend their time with. By then, girls have learned that bad boys are a lot like a really big roller coaster—nice to visit, but you wouldn't want to live there. And after too many trips around its twists and turns, you start getting dizzy and sick.

Until then, nice guys should learn to be charming and a little mysterious, and take advantage of the fact that nice girls love to have them as friends. While this may seem endlessly annoying, friendly girls are always a good source of dating advice and social networking.

Jenny Kane: I agree that what attracts nice girls to bad boys is the adventure, the unpredictability, the careless breaking of the rules. It's being with someone who has completely opposite ideals and morals than you. Sometimes nice guys become predictable and a little boring. Also, nice girls may not want to be with someone exactly like themselves. They long for something new and exciting. With a bad boy, you never know what's going to happen, so the girl will rarely be bored.

Some girls want to break out of their shells and are attracted to those guys who encourage them to take risks—guys who'll see them in a different light. After getting doted upon like a princess and behaving well for so long, there's a part of you that longs for someone who doesn't care. It's a yearning to ignore the rules, to do things that your parents always warned you not to do.

My advice to nice girls is to realize that inside every guy there can be a bad boy side, so don't just let someone go because he seems too nice. You may be surprised by what could happen. Just remember that the real bad boys can be dangerous. You may be attracted to them, but they'll get you into more trouble than they're worth.

At a Distance

Dear Dr. Wes and Ben,

I've been dating a girl for a year and a half. This week, we learned for sure that we're going to separate colleges in the fall. We knew this was going to happen and just ignored it, but now it's bringing back other past breakups we've each had and it makes me feel like I don't want to get involved with anyone like this again. It just ends in huge disappointment. Do you have any advice?

Ben Markley: I suppose my job is to play up the practical side of things, and frankly, these kinds of stories often end badly. Logistically, I should probably tell you to break things off.

I can't bring myself to do that, though. Don't get me wrong, I've read the end of Romeo and Juliet. Love is hard; what's more, it's scary, and we're bad at it. Nobody wants to invest in a tragedy, so many of us keep love on the shelf. When we do give it a try, we often find ourselves either blind to or skittish about the obstacles. Neither characteristic befits love.

Don't let the inevitability of this relationship's end keep you from living it out to the fullest.

Your dilemma here is not a logistical one; it's about commitment. This obstacle is not an inherently bad thing; some of the strongest relationships I know have gone through this, but it's hard. There's no such thing as a casual long-distance relationship, so you want to discuss this with each other and those close to you before you decide whether you really want to go through this. Feeling that you two are meant to be together doesn't guarantee a happy ending, but it's got to count for something.

Dr. Wes: Okay, I'll be the practical one, even as I'd rather just go along with Ben and support the romantic ideal. Yes, feeling "meant to be together" counts for something. This relationship has obviously been a key part of your high school years, and you'll carry it in your heart for the rest of your life. It will define a big part of who you were in your late teens and inform your future relationships, providing a unique and special memory to look back on with joy.

If you ask me, that's a big load for one relationship, so your job for now is to let it be enough. You could make a commitment and hang in there as Ben suggests, but in doing so you'll experience a high "opportunity cost" in terms of other relationships and experiences.

No matter what, don't stop reaching out and giving love a chance, and don't let the inevitability of this relationship's end keep you from living it out to the fullest while you can. And let me save you a little suspense by promising that you *will* go through this again. Probably several times. That's what it takes to find the right life partner, an ongoing search and a fair amount of trial, error and heartbreak. If it were easy, more people would get it right the first time.

And who knows? If you two really are "meant to be together," then you can each afford to go your separate ways and then check back later, when you've accumulated more time living. Sometimes things do come full circle, but don't try and force that too soon, lest you confine one another to a commitment that could quickly become more like a cage than a partnership.

Ill-Defined

Dear Dr. Wes and Samantha,

What should you do if you and your boyfriend break up and both of you want to get back together, but you don't really do it. You just end up secretly dating until one of you gets the nerve to stand up and truly ask?

Dr. Wes: Ah, the secret high school relationship. It sounds so romantic to steal away for a private moment of love, hidden from the intrusive eyes of peers and family who always seem to be up in your business. Unfortunately, I don't buy it. Just another ill-defined relationship in the new world of non-dating. I've threatened to develop a scale of teen and young adult relationships and hang it in my office. The left point would be "Friends who don't hold hands," and the right would be "Married." Twenty years ago, such a scale would fit on an 8½ x 11 inch sheet of paper laid sideways. Now it would take the whole fourteen-foot wall to include every point in-between.

Based on your description, I'm not even sure where your relationship would fall on that enormous scale. As best I can tell, you and your guy are still involved—he just won't claim you. That's one of the most hurtful relationship styles imaginable, where you're half in and half out. So, step up and ask the question. Then, if he says, "No, I really like this deal where I get the benefits and don't have to make any kind of commitment," boot him. If he instead says, "Okay. If it's important to you then it's important to me. Let's go public," I say great. You've taken the risk and it paid off. Either way, you win. Something happens.

I realize this isn't as easy as I make it sound. Just remember that you're practicing for your future relationships. In this one, you're either practicing passive behavior—letting life happen to you instead of acting on it—or you're getting taken advantage of.

If a secret relationship appeals to you, it means you're not quite ready for a legitimate relationship. Neither of you is willing to put yourself out there.

Boys have a hell of a good deal these days. I know this because they (and the girls they're with) tell me so. Girls imagine they've taken charge of their sexuality, when they've actually given up a lot of influence over their partners. While that may sound terribly sexist, the reality is that boys are going to behave just about as well as girls expect them to.

Sure, if you push your guy to be more serious, he may take off. But honestly, what will you have lost?

Samantha Schwartz: While there may be a thrill in avoiding commitment by having a "secret" relationship, it's like a great tap dancer performing in ballet shoes. It's nice, but it could have been excellent. The audience is confused and the dancer knows she could have done better. A secret relationship makes things awkward for you, your family and your friends because everyone is trying to decipher where you stand.

Your hesitation is likely merited. If a secret relationship appeals to you, it means you're not quite ready for a legitimate relationship. Neither of you is willing to put yourself out there.

When you break up, it's important to have some time to debrief the relationship. Whether you labeled the breakup as "mutual" or not, you both probably felt hurt and loss. I'm sure you both came up with reasons why you shouldn't be together. Think them over. Which ones were rational? If you don't discuss exactly why you broke up, you could end up facing all of the same problems again if you did ever get back together.

Also, think about timing. Have you given yourself enough time to truly see your life without him, or are you just falling back into the familiar comfort zone of having him around? Time away from a relationship is not about a certain number of days. It's about rediscovering who you are without him and figuring out the role he played in your life. If you feel complete *without* your boyfriend, you're ready to be with him. A great relationship is not based on completing each other, but on complimenting each other. Feel free to take some time to reflect. If you're meant to be together, he'll be willing to give you that time.

If you're truly set on being with him, tell him you want to get back together, and then set your conditions and listen to his. Discuss what each of you have to do to make the relationship work this time around.

Teen Community Property
and Pet Custody Battles

Dr. Wes: There's a growing trend among teen couples: attaining and joining assets. Kids seem to essentially move into each other's homes now, leaving behind clothes, keepsakes, notebooks, iPods, and other items of sentimental or economic worth. When the breakup comes, families have to go through the same maneuvers they would if their children were getting divorced. I've even seen law enforcement do civil standbys for teen property exchange.

Swapping a few sweatshirts, or exchanging DVDs, is a tolerable price to pay for romance, especially if both sets of parents are sensible and don't overreact. But the two areas that really bother me are phone contracts and pets. The cell phone situation is worst among newly minted eighteen-year-olds, who share their new adulthood with younger dating partners by getting a "family" phone plan. In other inexplicable cases, families actually sign the girl- or boyfriend onto their plans. I have one word of advice on this topic: Don't.

This goes for college-age kids, too. Unless you're living together and in a common-law marriage, there is nothing but heartache and expense for phone contracts, car payments, or other joint assets. And if you move ahead anyhow, be certain you have an escape plan in writing. Think of it as a "prenuptial" agreement without the nuptials.

Which brings us to the epidemic of teen couples getting joint pets. My advice here: Double-don't (with sugar on top). Just as a baby is ill-served by having very young, unmarried parents, no innocent pet is well-served in the middle of a teen romance. There's nearly a one hundred percent chance a teen couple will dissolve, leaving the partners in a pet custody battle or worse, one stuck with all the expense of ownership and no hope of "pet support."

Whenever you make something dependent on your dating relationship, you're building a house on a fault line.

Also, before taking on a pet, do a full accounting of future costs. I once spent $1,200 on my cat's thyroid. No, seriously. Imagine how it will be when you find you can't afford to keep your dog alive because you have to pay freshman housing deposit. Worse, by owning a pet, many young people either forfeit the chance to be in a sorority or live in the dorms, or have to pay expensive pet deposits. Others just leave the pet in the care of a parent, which kind of defeats the purpose.

Don't get me wrong. While it's very sweet that young couples want to share the intimacy of owning a pet or joining their resources for a common good, creating little marriages out of perfectly good teen love affairs can't help but end badly.

Ben Markley: I've been asked why people shouldn't break up through text. One big reason is that it leaves something behind. Friends who've been dumped that way know the wording of the text by heart and admit to reading it multiple times. If you can use a text to relive a breakup again and again, how terrible it must be to come home to an apartment you shared with your ex? Or worse, one you still share, because you can't get out of the lease. I don't mean to be pessimistic, but this is a serious issue to consider before you and your sweetheart go out and rent a place.

Whenever you make something dependent on your dating relationship, whether a phone, a pet, or an apartment, you're building a house on a fault line. A couple can be split; a pet can't. It throws a monkey wrench like no other into a separation. When two people are trying to part ways, this furry critter can make a clean break into a messy one. There's enough emotional rubble to sift through even without fighting over who gets the dog.

Wes is right: even leaving potential consequences aside, dating is no time to play marriage. One of its great benefits is that it allows partners to get to know each other without having to deal with the responsibilities of being a married couple.

Jealousy

Dear Dr. Wes and John,

I have a real problem with jealousy. It has gotten to the point where it makes me physically sick to see my boyfriend even talk with another girl for too long. I always worry that he is going to betray me, even though my friends tell me he won't.

John Murray: I know your friends have already told you this, but your boyfriend talking to other girls is not an indicator of whether he will leave you for one of them. One of my friends used to keep her boyfriend meticulously under watch. One day he announced he was through with her and found a new girl the same day. He didn't give any warning signs and my friend felt like she had been torpedoed. Couples who constantly worry about the state of their relationship are much less stable than those who take it a day at a time.

Do you know anyone who has a good relationship with someone they constantly snoopervise, control, and nag?

Remember that your boyfriend's opinion of you is not the standard to which you should hold yourself. In every middle or high school, there are smart, beautiful girls who never get asked out. The ones who let that fact hurt their self-esteem actually become less interesting to boys. When your relationship ends, as it probably will, you'll be left with yourself. Are you someone you want to be stuck with? The best girlfriends—and boyfriends, for that matter—make time to improve themselves by playing an instrument, learning a language, going out for a sport, etc. With these interests to fall back on, you won't be as scared that he will break up with you, which makes it less likely he will.

Talk to your boyfriend about your relationship, especially what you see as its goal, because if you don't know what each other wants, you'll be hard-pressed to find it. Are you just together for a fun time, or do you want a long term commitment? Develop a realistic understanding of what each of you is allowed to do with the opposite sex, and then stick to those rules. Some girls don't mind if their boyfriend flirts with the other girls, but if you're uncomfortable with that, your boyfriend should pay attention. In your case, however, let your boyfriend at least associate with other girls. Being with you can't eliminate his relationships with the rest of the world. Besides, I'm guessing that when your boyfriend talks to other females, he is reminded how you shine in comparison!

Dr. Wes: Jealousy is an anxiety-based emotion. I tell guys and girls there is exactly *nothing* they can do to control what their partner does when they're not around. N-O-T-H-I-N-G. The partner either believes cheating is okay or not, and then chooses whether to act on that belief. So, jealousy is one of the most useless emotions we've concocted. Think about it: do you know anyone who has a good relationship with someone they constantly snoopervise, control, and nag? Do you like it when your parents use those tactics to keep track of you?

Instead, try these things to reduce the chances of getting cheated on and hopefully redirect your anxiety in the process:

- **Pick someone who is generally trustworthy.** Pay attention to how your partner treats others. Many people date someone they know lies, steals, or does other disreputable things, and somehow expect to get better treatment themselves. Others cheat on their partners, then date the person they were cheating with and wonder why jealousy lies at the core of the relationship. I know you think you're the one special person he can be real with, but that just isn't happening.

- **Make your relationship the best it can be for your partner.** People like to be in relationships that meet their needs and they flee those that don't. Being overbearing and anxious will not make the relationship fun for either of you.

- **Be the partner you want to be with.** Some people are infuriated that their partner flirts with others, but seem to think it's fine if they do it themselves—or worse. Good old Sigmund Freud talked about projection. That's where people see in others their own worst characteristics and complain about them to conceal their own flaws. Before you can trust anyone else, you have to trust yourself and behave accordingly.

- **Give it some time before you get serious.** As people age, they get some of their wild oats sown, after which they become more interested in exclusive relationships.

I do feel for you. This is the age of anxiety for teens and young adults who want to be in serious relationships. *The Hookup Handbook* claims, "Girls are the new guys," meaning that girls are now more interested in short, emotionless relationships. Given the ease with which teens can find sexual outlets now, wanting to be in a trust-based relationship is bound to feel jittery at times.

Unless your partner is as dedicated to the relationship as you, there's nothing you can do to control him. If he's into you, enjoy it and force yourself to ignore your own anxiety.

If he's not, you know what to do.

Prom Invitation

Dear Dr. Wes and Samantha,

I'm a senior and have been dating the same girl for over two years. She is also a senior at our school, a delightful person, and just so happens to write a weekly advice column (but I don't want to give away her identity). Prom is coming up, and it's a really big deal for her and, by extension, me. She wants to be asked "creatively," so I was hoping the two of you could give me some suggestions. I think Samantha might just have a vested interest in this one, so I'm particularly interested to see what she has to say. Thanks for your help.

—Jon Cohen

Dr. Wes: Well, Jon, writing a letter to your girlfriend's advice column ranks among the most unique methods ever for asking someone to prom. Thanks for letting me in on such a sweet and romantic gesture.

Just so readers fully appreciate our little plan, the first Sam knew of this letter was Tuesday morning in the paper. Up to that point, she thought we were just churning out a generic column on prom dates! Although the letter writer won't benefit from her excellent advice (because he just got the job done), he'll probably do okay, assuming she doesn't say no.

Here's one bit of advice for all kids on this whole prom experience. There are plenty of nights out of the year to have a wild party, so try something different at prom. Go with all the majesty and pomp, and leave your wild side at home for a night. It'll be there when you need it. Back in the 1980s, I was in radio and had my own DJ system (no, seriously). I still remember the joy of watching young people on the most romantic night of their seventeen years.

You're all growing up fast. Make this night memorable, just as Samantha and Jon have already begun to do.

Samantha Schwartz: People are pairing up faster than Mahjong on level one. While not having a date isn't the end of the world, prom is one of the last chances to woo the person you've always had a thing for. Whether you're the asker or the replier, avoiding prom drama requires etiquette. And girls, it's the twenty-first century. YOU can be the asker.

Tips for asking:

- **Do your research.** Before you ask, find out whether the person you are asking already has a date. This information is easy to get from the person's friend who may even offer to help you plan how to ask.

- **Decide on your intentions.** You can have a great time at prom with a friend or a romantic date. Going with a friend is a great way to avoid prom drama. If you want to go with someone just as a friend, make sure you clarify this when you ask.

- **There's no "right" way to ask.** Some people are into the romantic thing, while others prefer something more creative or comedic. Still others would prefer that you just ask straight up. Hopefully, you know your potential date well enough to find the right approach.

- **Act fast!** The earlier you ask, the more likely you'll be to get a yes. This will also give you and your date time to find formal wear and arrange transportation and dinner.

Tips for replying:

- **Be kind.** Keep in mind that asking someone to prom involves taking a risk. The asker knows that, if you say "no," he will feel either devastated or, at the very least, embarrassed. Just because you have no interest in going to prom with the asker doesn't mean he or she needs to hear that stated so bluntly.

- **Don't be a prom player.** Some people treat being asked like an auction in which they award their company to the highest bidder. You may be tempted to hold out for a better offer. If you need time, tell the person you'll get back to him or her in one week. Any longer and the asker may lose a chance to take someone else. If you're waiting to be asked, take some action. Casually tell your ideal date that someone else asked you and you haven't decided on a reply yet.

- **Say "no" without making up a lie.** Don't tell the person you already have a date if you don't. You'll eventually be found out. Say, "No, thank you, but I am flattered that you asked." You don't have to offer apologies or long explanations. The more low-key your reply, the easier it is for the person to move on. Try not to tell everyone who asked you. It makes it much harder for that person to ask someone else.

- **Return the favor.** If you say "yes," make sure to show the person that you appreciate the invitation. Follow the asker's lead on prom plans, but offer your assistance whenever possible.

Not So Sweet Anymore

Dear Dr. Wes and Ben,

My boyfriend and I have been together for over seven months, and when we first went out in December, he was always texting me back to ask about my day. But now I sometimes send him a message without hearing back from him for hours or not at all. I've asked him about this and he always has an excuse. I tell him that he used to be really sweet to me and now he's not. What should I do?

Ben Markley: I remember a Calvin & Hobbes strip where Susie asks Calvin why he's so happy he got a 'C' on a test. He replies, "I find my life is a lot easier the lower I keep everyone's expectations." There's shelter in laziness. The more consistently lazy we are, the more shocking and awe-inspiring it is when we finally step up.

I say this so pointedly because my girlfriend had the same problem with me a few months ago. I'd be indifferent and distant for a few weeks, but then I'd do something incredibly sweet to try to make up for it. That's the thing about guys: we're doers. Sometimes we don't realize what a genuine compliment or a simple "How was your day?" can mean. We put those things on the backburner because we really don't realize that they matter.

My girlfriend snapped me out of my daze when she said, "You know, I liked when you used to be sweet instead of just doing sweet things." Tell your boyfriend about the little things that make you feel special. He might be surprised at just how easy it really is to do.

Texting has become the new way to gauge whether someone is really into you.

Dr. Wes: There are two intertwined issues here, one electronic and one emotional. Texting has become the new way to gauge whether someone is really into you. This gets to be a problem in part because of gender differences in texting behavior. From a sociological standpoint, women and teenage girls have always been interconnected in social networks in a different and more intimate way than guys. Now Facebook, Twitter, and texting have extended that network far beyond anything we imagined even five years ago.

Texting offers a new metaphor for relationships. Thumbs fly over the keyboard when you're trying to attract each other, moderate after the relationship is established and slow to a crawl when the love begins to slide. So, you're correct to wonder whether you and your guy are headed downhill. Except you don't really know, because the unfortunate side of texting and Facebook is that they actually limit communication by running it through a digital filter that cuts out body language, facial expression, and touch.

So, I agree with Ben. Take your question straight to the boy. Sit down and ask whether he thinks things are dying off or, perhaps worse, he sees everything as perfectly okay. If a couple doesn't share expectations for these things, they won't survive. And remember, the purpose of being in a relationship is to find out which people you're right with. That takes time and practice. Don't be afraid to fail. Having this talk with your boyfriend is good practice for all your future loves.

Having His Cake

Dear Dr. Wes and Samantha,

I found out my boyfriend cheated on his last girlfriend. He says it's because of how she treated him. Is it true that once a guy is a cheat he's always a cheat? I want to trust him, but don't want to get hurt.

Samantha Schwartz: Every situation is unique, and you need more information before you make any decisions. Tell your boyfriend you want to understand why and how he ended up cheating. You want to trust him and to learn more about his past. Give him a chance to state his case, but don't take everything he says at face value. Be like an airport security worker; let the majority of his story roll past you, but stop and ask questions when things seem suspicious.

Here are some key things to find out:

- **Frequency:** How many times did he cheat on his previous girlfriend? Did he cheat on other girls? Did he cheat toward the end of the relationship or all the way through? If he only cheated once and then decided he needed to break up with her, his conduct, while selfish, is more forgivable than if he strung her along while cheating on her multiple times. Also, find out when and where he cheated. That information may come in handy if you ever suspect he's cheating on you.

  If you're true love was a jerk to his ex-girlfriend, he's more likely to eventually treat you that way too.

- **Context:** Why did he cheat? How exactly did his ex treat him? Don't accept broad generalizations like "she hurt me" or "she said mean stuff to me." Ask for specific examples. Remember that abuse can be both physical and emotional in a relationship. While context might explain his misbehavior, it doesn't excuse it.

- **Who he cheated with:** Did he cheat with someone he's still in contact with? Are they now "just friends?" If so, he might cheat on you with this person. If he has no feelings for her, then he shouldn't be in regular contact with her.
- **Remorse:** How does he feel about what he did? If he has learned that cheating doesn't solve problems in a relationship and, in fact, is hurtful and dishonest, maybe he *has* learned something.

Most importantly, make it clear that you find cheating unacceptable and if he's thinking about cheating on you, you'd rather he just break up instead.

Dr. Wes: Well, this is a depressing topic only a week after Valentine's Day. While I like her strategies, Samantha is more forgiving than I am. Perhaps it's a generational thing. I see a lot of young people who recover from these boundary violations more quickly than we did. Or at least they think they do. I'm not so sure.

I get to spend a lot of time thinking about these kinds of things, so I have my share of little tips for the lovelorn. Here's one that fits your situation: Don't judge someone by how they treat the people they like. Judge them by how they treat the people they don't like. Later, this will translate into: Never marry anyone you don't want to be divorced from.

If you're true love was a jerk to his ex-girlfriend, then he's more likely to eventually treat you that way too. We like to ignore things at the beginning of a relationship, when everything is flowers and unicorns running through a field. But as love ages, the raw spots start to show through. Only then do you find out the true measure of your partner and the bond you've formed. If in the past, your guy handled relationship problems by cheating, there's a good chance you'll end up on the same end of that stick when he starts to like you less.

Samantha is right. There are always complications and contexts, but even if he dated the world's worst girlfriend, she did not deserve that kind of treatment. Breaking up beats the heck out of cheating, and guys and girls who don't stand up and make a decision are often trying to have their proverbial cake and eat it too. If that's what went on with this guy, I'd suggest keeping your cake to yourself.

That said, I do believe in redemption. If, as Sam notes, your guy now understands the damage cheating causes and can explain how he's changed, then *maybe* things will be different with you. Just don't cling too tightly to this hopeful ideal, desperately wanting to believe you're so much more special than the last girl, and that he would never treat you this way.

True Romance

Dear Dr. Wes and Samantha,

My boyfriend is really sweet and always nice to me, and we really love each other and I trust him. But we are really different. I'm interested in grades and school and want to be a vet someday. He doesn't try very hard, doesn't like school, plays a lot of computer games and smokes a lot of weed. I want to be with him, but I want to know whether he'll ever grow out of this lifestyle or not?

Dr. Wes: What do *Romeo and Juliet*, just about every book by Jane Austen, *Fiddler on The Roof*, and *Twilight* all have in common? A titanic struggle between the heart and mind in picking a good dating partner. And in nearly every fictional account, guess which wins? The heart. It makes a better story.

Now, back to real life. Yours. What should your head be thinking? I have my own little proverb for those wanting better love: Never form a relationship with someone you wouldn't consider marrying. I'm not suggesting you plan your wedding at sixteen, but teen relationships can be strong predictors of how you'll couple later on, so we want you to get it right. Practically speaking, is this guy someone you'd want to marry and have kids with? It doesn't sound like it from your letter. Or, if you don't like that angle, ask yourself whether he's the kind of guy you'll want your daughter dating in twenty years. I'm guessing that's a big "no" too.

Maybe it makes more sense to find a guy with little or no assembly required.

It's almost Christmas and I'm not trying to be the Scrooge of love here. I just think we need to balance all those deep feelings with some practical attention to detail. Why limit yourself to a guy whom you *just* love? Why not shoot for the whole deal: Love, ambition, a life focused on something other than *World of Warcraft* and pot? You do well in school and have some pretty big goals. Expand your horizons and shoot for someone who can share that part of your life too.

I see in your letter that you're asking yourself that one magnificent question: Will he change? I have the definitive answer: Why wait to find out? I've seen a lot of sketchy kids turn themselves into pretty great adults. Some don't get there until their thirties. More than a few never come around. The question your head needs to be asking your heart is whether right here and now you should spend your time with someone who isn't really going anywhere. You can always find him ten years from now on Facebook and see how he's turned out.

Sure, you could give him your list of must haves and can't stands, and see whether he rises to the occasion. That's worked for a lot of girls in real life and it always works well in romantic fiction. People do change for each other. If they didn't, few marriages would ever last. But you have to start with a pretty good core and then work like hell as a team, not just you nitpicking at him and him trying endlessly to please you. Maybe it makes more sense to find a guy with little or no assembly required.

It's not what you want to hear, but I hope you'll give this some thought. You're young. Enjoy practicing.

Samantha Schwartz: It seems like you enjoy being around your boyfriend and you care about him quite a bit. But, as you've noticed, you're headed down different paths. While a friend with a devil-may-care attitude can be exciting, having a boyfriend with that lifestyle will become more burdensome than fun.

You seem like a goal-oriented, hardworking girl. Date someone who will motivate and encourage you, not draw you into a tangled web of distractions. Share your dreams with him and hear his in return. Girls mature faster than boys, so in a few years your boyfriend could turn his life around, just as Wes suggests. He could become a driven, successful guy that you admire.

But you can't *make* that happen. If he wants to become a different person, you can support him, but it must be his choice. Couples only stretch each other to become better people after they start out as equals. Think about it like stretching a sheet over the bed with someone. If you pull too hard on your side, their side snaps back in your face.

Don't be a badgering, demanding girlfriend, putting a huge strain on your relationship. Just break up with this guy in a gentle, kind way so that you can still be friends. Tell him you think he's great and you love being around him, but you just have different goals, and you don't want to force him to be someone he's not. Be wary of promises that he will change for you. Instead, say that if you see he's changed over time, you might consider dating him again.

St. Valentine's Day Lament

Dear Dr. Wes and Marissa,

As a teenage boy who has never had a girlfriend, let me ask you something about Valentine's day. How many depressed teens do you encounter on this great "feel-like-crap-if-you-are-single" day?

Dr. Wes: Forty-two! There are exactly forty-two depressed single teens on any given Valentine's Day, which not incidentally is the answer to life, the universe, and everything, as fans of *Hitchhiker's Guide to the Galaxy* know. Seriously, what you are really asking is whether V-day is all it's cracked up to be as far as romance is concerned.

Your letter suggests what I hear from many clients each February, that Valentine's Day is better named "Single Awareness Day," because it puts a greater focus on relationships, and those who aren't in one tend to compare themselves with those who are. A great deal of the therapy I do with teenagers and young adults is helping them learn how to love and be loved by others. So, this is a pretty big issue.

Set a goal to make next year's Valentine's Day far less crappy than this one. There are just as many lonely teenage girls out there as there are boys, maybe more. Your job is to set up a plan to find them. Contrary to popular belief, "hanging out" and going to wild drunken parties doesn't

One should never feel like they need to have a relationship to be happy.

necessarily access the best dating pool. Instead, figure out what you're good at. If you do well in clubs or youth groups, enroll in the largest one you can find. When you hit eighteen, there are online dating services that work well for many young adults, especially the shy ones. If you're a gamer, get involved with the groups that have both guys and girls. In short, find your dating pool.

While searching, bone up on exactly who you are. This may seem kind of obvious, but it's not. Some young men have a very distorted view of themselves and can't figure out why others don't relate to them. If you have a nice sister or (girl) friends, ask for an honest appraisal. You may need to change your clothes, manners, grooming, pick up lines, etc. Also, do some deeper self-reflection on what you believe, what you want in life, and so on.

Of course, this is less important if you're just trying to hook up, but in this column we tend to favor the more serious approaches to dating. So, try getting real with yourself and things may go better.

Marissa Ballard: The exact number is unknown to me, but I have to imagine that there are many more than forty-two. Though Valentine's Day gives more attention to couples, any holiday can get a single person feeling down.

If your main goal is to find someone to spend the next V-day with, I'll share the top three things I think young men our age should be doing differently:

- **Talk about feelings.** I spoke to a male friend of mine just the other day and he was saying how he and the girl that he was interested in never talked about their feelings. It seems to be the general misperception that if a guy expresses his emotions girls will think he's gay. Gay or straight, girls like to know that you have feelings. Showing them will only make the relationship better.

- **Stop playing games.** A lot of people I know are really into playing games when it comes to starting a relationship, subtly trying to make the other person jealous for example. Believe me, the kind of girl you want will not put up with that kind of behavior and you shouldn't either.

- **Cut the stereotypes.** There are too many generalizations about women floating around. No matter what magazines and TV tell you, not all girls are the same. It is just as silly to assume all men are alike. This means that you cannot go into a date or relationship expecting to know how it will turn out, and remaining bitter about a past relationship will pretty much doom your next.

Finally, one should never feel like they need to have a relationship to be happy. Plenty of people are doing just fine without a significant other. Still, having someone there to talk to and depend on, other than family, can be wonderful.

Even if you didn't have anyone to share this Valentine's Day with, I can guarantee that you will have someone for a future one.

Living Together?

Dear Dr. Wes and Ben,

I want to live with my boyfriend next year when we both go to college. My parents are actually okay with it because we've been together since ninth grade and he's like a member of our family, but he didn't seem very excited about this idea. After I dragged it out of him, he admitted he doesn't want to live with me because he's afraid it will ruin our relationship. I think we're ready to take our relationship to the "next level," as they say. It's causing nothing but arguments now, so we agreed to get your advice and we'll probably go with whatever you say.

Dr. Wes: Well, thanks for the confidence you've vested in us, but in the end you'll have to make the decision. We get the easy job, handing out advice. You get the hard one, living with your choices. So, choose wisely.

I call the kind of dating you've done in high school "radical monogamy," and I generally prefer it to the hookup culture, yet it does have its limits. Hoping that your relationship will survive the transition to college is admirable, but it comes at a time when the world is opening up and inviting you to expand your horizons.

I'm not suggesting that you break up, especially since you're going to the same school. But I'm not sure you should escalate things right now, either. Your boyfriend is pretty astute in realizing that living together does *not* take you to the next step of romance. It takes you to a whole new and complicated world of roommating. Living with anyone is about two things: conflict and problem-solving. Done well, it can teach you a lot about others but even more about yourself. But few of us did that well on our first or second try. In your first years of college, you're better off trying out your cohabitation skills on someone who doesn't matter that much to you—not a best friend and certainly not a long-term boyfriend.

If one of you feels forced into this arrangement, then living together doesn't make much sense.

In a worst-case scenario, you and your boyfriend may find that college creates a natural drift away from one another. I know you don't want to think that way, but it's at least a possibility. Just imagine what will happen if you break up while living together? The awkwardness and pain will be right up in your face every day.

Ben Markley: Before I write a column, I always play my guitar to clear my mind. This week, it actually helped me with my answer. I love my guitar, but I hate tuning it. I can have five strings in perfect harmony with each other, but if one is even a little flat, it makes every chord I play painful to the ears. No matter how skillfully I play, it's going to sound bad. I don't know the details of your situation, but I do know one important fact: one of your strings is out of tune. Your boyfriend isn't confident about living with you at this point.

It would be overly optimistic to assume that simply going for it would relieve his reservations. It doesn't matter who brings doubt into the situation, since you'll both have to deal with it if you decide to live together. Sure, there's a good chance you could work it out as roommates, but that's no cakewalk. Tuning is hard enough by itself; imagine having to tune while you're playing a song.

Bottom line: If one of you feels forced into this arrangement, then living together doesn't make much sense right now. It would definitely have a profound effect on your relationship, good or bad, but college is an experience with plenty of potential to develop your relationship all by itself. Your boyfriend might fall in tune with living together in the future, but until then, there are plenty of other songs you can play.

Crazy Love

Dear Dr. Wes and John,

For a long time now I have liked a guy. We have the same interests, and we used to flirt and hang out with each other a lot. He told me he didn't want a girlfriend and I was fine with that, so we still hung out about once or twice a month. It isn't much, I know. Now, I find myself attached to him emotionally, which scares me because I know he doesn't feel the same way. I've tried everything to stop myself—I even read *He's Just Not That Into You*. Nothing works. The more time passes, the more I feel as if I am that crazy girl who likes him. I don't want to be her.

Dr. Wes: Love has a bad reputation of being a bit crazy-making. I prefer thinking of it as something we choose to give to others for good and sensible reasons. Then again, I'm forty-four. At your age, love is much more emotional—dark and beautiful, excruciating and euphoric, stellar and hellish. Anything with such kick has the potential for obsession. I doubt you're that far gone, but it may feel as if you are.

Unfortunately, our culture has a long literary tradition of glorifying obsessive love. How many movies include a smitten guy (or girl) desperately pursuing one true love and, in the final scene, winning her over with sheer force of will? In the real world, that's a good way to get labeled as a stalker, or as you put it "the crazy girl that likes him." It's not a pathway to healthy romance.

Don't sleep too many times with a guy you don't want to fall in love with.

Sit down and ask yourself some questions:

What am I getting out of this relationship? Is there something lacking elsewhere in my life—emotion, drama, companionship, attention? People don't do much of anything without reasons or motivations. If this relationship is meeting some hidden need, maybe you can meet it elsewhere.

Isn't there someone else to date? This is not the only guy in your school or the world. Decide to start other relationships whether that "feels right" or not (it won't). See if they don't distract and then divert you from this one. It may sound like nothing but a rebound, but rebounds usually resolve lost love, or else they wouldn't be so popular. Act "as if" things are okay and, shockingly enough, they will become so.

What about intimacy? Here's a piece of advice I got from sex therapist Laura Berman of Chicago: *Don't sleep too many times with a guy you don't want to fall in love with.* For women, sex is ultimately about emotional interchange. If you and your friend are intimate, it's going to become increasingly hard to let go.

Enjoy this time of life in which love is a flaming blowtorch that sometimes leaves one singed. Just remember not to base any big decisions on it or commit yourself to it. In the long run, that torch won't fuel a relationship. Maturity and a good match will. Keep looking.

John Murray: Chances are you already know what to do. You know your friend isn't interested in romance but is okay with friendship. It's really your call as to what to do next. There are lots of times when "just friends" works out well and I believe yours is one of these cases.

Actually, you're a long way from becoming the "crazy girl" with a one-way crush. It's perfectly healthy to talk to your friend twice a month—if that's what you want. If you still enjoy each other's presence, and you can avoid bringing up romance, then spend as much time together as you're both comfortable with. Just avoid flirting or hinting about future love, otherwise you'll just live out the same drama over and over again. Limit how many text messages you send him to avoid coming across as obsessive. And if your friendship begins to bring you more misery than fun, it might be time to break off communications altogether.

My friends and I have fierce debates on what makes a woman attractive and we've finally reached a conclusion: There is no gold standard to which women can be compared. Different guys are into different girls and there's not much we can do about it. Of course, you could try and become what you think your friend desires in order to attract him, but then you'd risk losing a part of yourself. A better solution is to actively search for new friends, while keeping an eye out for a real boyfriend. I can personally attest that there is something of a placebo effect involved in infatuation. If you think there's no one more handsome than your friend, your eyes won't want to prove you wrong.

Finally, guys tend to focus their groups on activities, while girls focus their activities on groups. So, a guy might call his friends to play a game of basketball, while a girl might meet up with her friends and decide what to do together. This can cause confusion when the sexes get together. You implied that you simply "hung out" with your friend, but what was he actually doing? Watching TV? Surfing the web? Playing video games? Or was he interacting with you?

Your goal is to have friends who relate to you and do activities you can enjoy together.

Breaking Up is (Unnecessarily) Hard to Do

Dear Dr. Wes and Samantha,

My relationship with my boyfriend isn't going very well. We fight all the time and both of us have found ourselves talking to other people, but somehow we always end up back together. I want us to be friends after we break up. We really love each other but somehow that doesn't make it work out.

Dr. Wes: If you really intend to break up, then I have a radical idea for you. Break up. One of the most common problems of couples today isn't being together. It's getting apart. I'm not sure how this came about over the last fifteen years, but young people have come to believe that couples should just slide gracefully into friendship after they split up.

To this I ask one simple question. Why? If you and your guy aren't doing well as a couple, why prolong the agony and try to stay friends? I know it's not as easy as I make it sound, but I've had this conversation literally 2,000 times and it's not as hard as you think. This is a big world and there are multitudes of people to get to know. Here are my tips:

- **Say goodbye face-to-face.** Forget texting back and forth or changing Facebook statuses as a sign that you're through. Saying it in person makes it more real, even if you have to do it in public to be certain things go okay. Occasionally, breakups actually get dangerous, so go out to lunch. Once you're there, eat, get it said, set the rules of disengagement, and leave. No long goodbye kisses, or anything else, because nothing good comes of breakup sex.
- **Run. Run like the wind.** Agree to end all contact for at least ninety days. If you're lab partners or doing a class project together, beg the teacher to let you split off. I don't recommend

changing class schedules mid-term, but do what you can to avoid each other next semester. Less pain and more gain.

- **Return all the "stuff."** Give back his things immediately via your mutual friends—shirts, rings, puppies, concert tickets, everything that belongs to him. Don't argue about any of it. If your boyfriend gave it to you and he wants it back, make it happen. Nobody is going to care in ten years if you hung on to his letter jacket or ring. Except maybe your husband.

- **Hit delete.** Today, breakup means purging each other from your phone and Facebook. Or program your phone to say "Don't Answer" when his number rings, a handy reminder in our high tech age. Some teens prefer entering something less flattering, but that's up to you.

- **Get your friends on message.** If your ex approaches them to relay something to you, have them politely explain that you've moved on and ask them not to tell you about it.

- **Enlist support.** Family and social support, or even a counselor, can help when the going gets rough (and it will). It may seem surprising that teen and young adult breakups are now fodder for therapy, but it's one of the most common problems we see today.

Every relationship is a learning experience and so is every breakup. Work hard on both.

Let yourself experience what it feels like to be independent.

Samantha Schwartz: Time to stop floating through your tumultuous relationship, letting the waves of romantic conflict break on you. Jump ship. Don't be mean or point out his flaws. Don't feel like you need to list the reasons. It's fine to say it's just not working.

Many people stay in relationships that are just "okay" because they're afraid to leave someone they've grown accustomed to, missing out on exciting new relationships. Don't start anything right away, because you should both take time for yourselves. In fact, try to avoid dating for at least a month or two, after the breakup.

As Wes notes, when the wounds are fresh and you're both vulnerable, you could easily slip back into your usual habits, so avoid contact. Worse, if you keep processing the breakup together, you could get into an argument that prevents you from ever being friends. If you happen to run into each other, be cordial but avoid calling, texting or hanging out alone. Force yourself to "just say no" whenever you're tempted to sip from the stalker cup. Don't read his Facebook page, see his plans to go to a restaurant, and then just happen to show up.

Assigning custody of the friends can be tricky, too. Avoid drama by only inviting a few of your common friends to hang out at a time, and don't arrange everyone-but-the-ex plans. If you end up having no choice but to hang out in a big group, say "hi" to your ex, but don't spend the evening with him. Focus on your other friends instead. Further, don't bash him in public. When you get really frustrated, sit down and write him a letter about everything that's angering you. Vent all your mean, hurtful thoughts and feelings. *Then, DON'T send the letter.*

Let yourself experience what it feels like to be independent. Learn something new that you never had time to try before. Refresh your relationships with friends and family. The busier you are, the less likely you'll be to snap back to your ho-hum relationship. By becoming a better, stronger, more confident version of yourself, you're in a much better position to have a healthy friendship with your ex.

3 SEX

Promiscuous

Dear Dr. Wes and John,

I've had the same friends since grade school. Now that we're in middle school their morals have really changed. Many are getting really promiscuous and I don't know what to do with them. I know I don't have to follow them, but I'm just really tired of watching them throw themselves away like this. We're only in ninth grade.

Dr. Wes: I see many kids in both your situation and that of your friends. In my view, our sexual revolution has devolved from something liberating in the 1960s to a new millennium where sex simply isn't taken seriously. For this column, let's ignore the question of whether your friends are ready to be doing this at fifteen (they aren't), and focus on "what to do with them," by offering a best practices model of teen sexuality. This requires three components:

- Protecting the body from disease
- Protecting the future from unwanted pregnancy
- Protecting the heart from regret

We've made it easy for teens to master the pregnancy component. Between condoms, hormone-based birth control, and emergency contraception, there isn't a good statistical reason for anyone to experience unwanted pregnancy. Accidents happen, but if one is as cautious as they should be (e.g., using both condoms and hormone-based contraceptive), the risk is greatly reduced. Disease is another matter. Most sexually active girls will have some strain of HPV by the time they are twenty. Many will have contracted herpes or another STD, none of which are hard to catch.

However, what your letter proposes is carelessness with the third component—protecting the heart. Few would argue that we live in a culture that values the intimacy and importance of sexuality. I agree that by becoming "promiscuous" in middle school, your friends are throwing something away. By randomly hooking up or rushing to sexual engagement in serial relationships, they're doing a lot more than risking disease and pregnancy. They're risking a young adulthood full of regrets. I know this because I see young people in their mid-twenties, mostly women, who look back on ten years of sexual careless-ness with great disappointment. Some of those memories so upset and embarrass them that they seem traumatized in much the same way victims of sexual abuse have been. That may sound extreme, but I've found it to be true many times over.

> *Because real gentlemen are in short supply, many girls settle for less than they deserve.*

I'm not telling anyone when, if, or how to behave sexually. Each of us has to make that decision for ourselves. Most teens will become sexually active before young adulthood. My only wish is that you use this time to make some good memories, rather than a lot of really bad ones.

Your friends are headed into the latter category and I am glad you're questioning how they're handling their sexuality.

John Murray: Our society is starved for intimacy. Surveys indicate the average American has only two close friends, and one in four report having no one with whom they can discuss important issues. This is twice the number reported twenty years ago. Middle school can be a particularly lonely time. Mine certainly was. For lonely people, sex can provide an illusion of intimacy. During sex, the hormone oxytocin is released to act as psychological superglue between you and your sexual partner. That works great if you're married or in a serious relationship, but it comes down like a rock if you're just dating. Even after a couple feels it's time to move on, they still have a powerful bond between them. That's why you see couples constantly break up and come back together again long after their relationship has deteriorated. And when multiple partners are involved, your psyche gets confused about who it's supposed to be bonded with. After years of promiscuity, you're tied in a web of conflicting feelings pulling you apart.

Fortunately, simply by being a friend, you can help your peers understand that an intimate relationship need not be a sexual one. At the risk of sounding touchy-feely, I'd suggest you hug them more. People need to be touched twenty times a day, but most Americans get far less. If our society was more European in its attitude about touching, we'd probably feel less lonely. You can also show your friends an alternative by example. Most teenagers overestimate the sexual activity of their peers. Your friends will pay attention if they see you finding happiness in a chaste relationship.

When the time is right, talk to them about their sexuality. They won't admit it, but I doubt they really enjoy behaving promiscuously. Because real gentlemen are in short supply, many girls settle for less than they deserve. Tell your friends they're worth more than their partners are giving them. In fact, they're worth so much that they don't even need a relationship. Try to rekindle their sense of hope. Though there are plenty of eels in the sea, there will always be real men who understand respect.

Too Young?

Dear Dr. Wes and Julia,

How young is too young for sex?

Dr. Wes: I'm tempted to paraphrase an old adage and suggest that if you have to ask, you probably are. However, that answer's a bit too pithy to do justice to an honest and valid question. Unfortunately, nobody really likes this one because we're all sure we know the answer, but when pressed to explain ourselves, we tend to fumble.

There are several levels of concern here. The first one is legal. The cold fact is that if you're under the age of consent[4] you can't legally have

---

[4] Check your state statutes! Every state has a different age of consent, and some have two different levels, depending on the age of the partner.

sex. Of course, there are big problems with such laws, particularly deciding who gets charged if both teens are underage. I've seen it go both ways, but historically the guy has gotten the brunt end of the law. Today, just as many girls are interested in sex as guys, and some are pretty pushy, so it's hard to find a victim and an offender in most of these encounters. Try hard to avoid being either one. And when it comes to charging a crime, you'd be surprised what constitutes sex. It is *not* just intercourse. So, my advice to you from a legal standpoint is to wait until you reach the age of consent in your state.

Now, before you wonder where I got my PhD in naïveté, I am well aware that many teens are already sexually involved and quite a few are under their state's age of consent. Most don't give a crap about that law, even if they should.

So, I'd ask you to consider something more complicated than your actual (chronological) age—your emotional maturity. From a developmental standpoint, few teens are emotionally ready to be sexually involved. Of course, that's not stopping anyone either, but it's worth thinking about in making a decision.

Consider whether you'll be happy with your decision a month, a year, or five years from now. Will you want to tell your children about this decision someday when they ask? Or will you be ashamed of the choice because you look back and wish you'd waited for a better relationship with someone you really loved.

Julia Davidson: This question reminds me of a song from a musical my high school put on a few years ago. The eighth grade girl characters sang, "How far is too far?" as an introduction to their first sex education class. The song never answered the question, but implied this to be a very personal decision.

I would define "too young for sex" as a person who is uneducated about, unprepared for, or not able to consent to sex. Once all of those categories are overcome and *hopefully* the parents are aware of the child's actions, sex becomes an option. That *doesn't* mean that by reading a pamphlet, going on the pill and using a condom you're automatically ready, nor should you have to be. Sex is not a right of initiation or the latest trend. It's something intimate and it should be respected as such.

Another thing overlooked, as hormones begin to override common sense, is consequence, STDs, pregnancy, the disappointed look on your parents' faces. Disregarding a clear, well-thought-out decision to remain abstinent could result in a lot worse consequences than simply not having sex.

Prude?

Dear Dr. Wes and Julia,

When I entered seventh grade, I became more comfortable with the whole idea of dating. But the more guys I got to know, the more I was being asked the same question over and over. Before the guy made up his mind about going out with me, he would ask whether or not I was "prude." If I said yes, then he wouldn't go out with me. If I said "no," then I was giving him the wrong impression. It seems like a guy's whole decision is based on that one question. Worse, I'm not sure exactly what "prude" even means. Are all girls in middle and high school being put under the same stress because they aren't sure how to answer the question?

Dr. Wes: I did some expert research on this blunt little gem and found the exact language more of a middle school thing, so it may diminish after you get to high school. Yet, I also found an even more direct version of this question when querying college girls. At that age, guys simply ask if the girl "is a sexual person" or something along those lines. My informants say that being "prude" really has no clear definition. It could mean refusing to engage in any sexual behavior, from making out to full-on intercourse.

Putting a girl through an interview to see if she'll put out is pretty sketchy.

In fact, one of the biggest problems I see among teens is a complete lack of clarity and definition in sexual relationships. One person's "making out" is another person's "pretty close to sex" if you get my drift. So, if I were you, I'd be interviewing my potential boyfriends just as rigorously as they seem to want to interview you. There's nothing wrong with getting the boundaries and intentions straight up front, and that means having a clear picture of what each of you is talking about. Remember, nothing is ever what it is—it's the meaning we give it. So, your job is to figure out for each and every person who asks, what it is that they consider prudish and then decide whether you want to be with that person.

Putting a girl through an interview to see if she'll put out is pretty sketchy, especially if the only answer he'll accept is "Sure, I'd love to do it with you. Meet me at five." I'm probably getting old, but I yearn for the days when boys had to work at it a little bit. At this point, far too many girls aren't taking such questions as seriously as you are. So guess what? Boys aren't either. Your letter suggests we're really moving into a kind of market-based dating culture where you demand to know exactly what you're getting before you commit yourself.

While a frank discussion of these issues is valuable in any relationship, getting rejected because you won't perform as some guy wants you to is degrading to both you and him. So, I applaud you for having the courage to question this.

You may end up with fewer boyfriend notches on your belt, but each relationship you do have will be a better experience.

Julia Davidson: I did my own research and found two very different definitions:

> *"Prude: a person who is excessively proper or modest in speech, conduct, dress, etc." (dictionary.com); "Prude: a guy or girl who's afraid to do anything sexual or kinda shy around the opposite sex" (urbandictionary.com)*

I would consider myself something pretty near a prude—the former definition, not the latter. I am reserved and modest in my ways, was raised to be a polite person and I respect myself for it. However, as with the phrases "hook up" or "conservative," prude's meaning has moved from something that was once considered respectable to some sort of classification system.

"Are you a prude?" is really just a cowardly way for someone to question your sexual feelings, intentions, and promiscuity. It makes the guy asking feel safe because it turns something complicated into a yes or no question, with no feelings involved. Even if it isn't asked in this manner, this question has, is, and will always be asked by people too immature or inexperienced to phrase it any other way.

While it is a rude way to ask, the guy is probably not intending to hurt your feelings but rather to simply protect his own. One way to deflect this question is by taking the high road and ending the conversation, saying you aren't comfortable being asked that sort of thing at this early point in your relationship. This kind of response can itself mark you as a "prude," but if that means you're a mature, levelheaded person who is aware of her own standards, then so be it. Outside influence and indirect questions should not pressure you away from your own expectations of yourself or others.

Too Serious?

Dear Dr. Wes and Ben,

My parents don't like that I've been dating the same guy since September. They think we're "too serious" and that we "spend too much time together." They won't let me hang out with him as much as I want, but they let me hang out with other people. My grades are good and I'm a sophomore, so I think they are being strict for no reason. Do they want me to be like my friends and get with a new guy every week?

Ben Markley: Commitment is a great thing. Clinginess is not. I don't know what your relationship is like, so maybe I'm wasting my ink, but there are a lot of high school relationships that mistake "commitment" for simply being together all the time. We've all seen a "whipped" boyfriend or the "obsessed" girlfriend whose weekend plans can turn on a dime if their significant other has an idea. Unfortunately, we're often blind to this development when we're experiencing it.

Your folks need to spend some time updating their understanding of how teenagers couple these days.

Maybe you're right and your parents are being unreasonable, but consider what your relationships look like to them. Where do your friends fit into your life right now? Would you be spending time with them if your time with your boyfriend wasn't being limited? If not, then maybe your parents are trying to get you to see something you struggle to see yourself. Maybe "too serious" isn't so much about your relationship as it is about the effect your boyfriend is having on the rest of your life.

We should always be willing to take a second to step back, take a look, and be honest with ourselves. Such candid reflection will help you, your boyfriend, and your parents down the road.

Dr. Wes: Having taken this journey more than twice with teens, I think you and Ben may not be reading the full meaning behind your parents' concern. Usually, this parental worry comes from two false beliefs: that too much time together increases the likelihood that teens will become sexually active; and/or teens are better off with multiple relationships before settling into anything too serious.

At the risk of sounding crass, if time for sex is the goal, it doesn't take much for teens to find their way, and far too few confine sexual expression to monogamous relationships. So, if your parents are actually trying to engineer your dating habits toward the "less serious," they may be promoting something very different than what they intend—hooking up without commitment or intimacy. While I agree that everyone needs a balance of dating exploration and exclusivity in adolescence, your folks need to spend some time updating their understanding of how teenagers couple these days.

If you think I'm supporting your position on this, you're right. Radical coupledom at your age isn't perfect, but if given the choice between that and the twenty-first century version of "dating around," I gotta go with your theory hands down.

Cost-Benefit

Dear Dr. Wes and Miranda,

Every time my boyfriend and I are making out, he brings up sex. He asks whether the conversation bothers me, and I always say no, because it normally doesn't. Until last night. He knows I don't want to have sex before marriage, but he said jokingly, "Well, maybe I'll change your mind." The more we talk about sex—like what it means to each of us and stuff—the more desensitized I get to the idea of doing it. So, one night, he asked if I honestly thought that we would never have sex before marriage. For some reason, I said "No." So, he asked when and I finally said "Six to nine months." He seemed kind of saddened, so I asked whether it was a deal breaker. He said it wasn't, but that after nine months he would want to have a serious conversation about why I wouldn't want to. I am so confused right now. He treats me really well, makes me feel like I'm the only girl in the room. I feel like this shouldn't be that hard for him, and it freaks me out that I'm even considering having sex with him.

Miranda Davis: Your boyfriend is probably a great guy and I have no doubt that you're honestly and accurately describing the way he treats you. But at the same time, he is a teenage boy. I'm not excusing his behavior, but be aware that every single hormone-raging boy is similar when it comes to sex. He can be a model student and sweet about everything, but he'll always want to have sex when put into an intimate situation.

I'm not telling you to jump into bed with him just because he's a normal boy. I assume you're choosing to wait for a reason, and that is perfectly okay. Anyone who says it isn't is wrong. It doesn't matter what your reasoning is, or the logic behind it—if you feel that you don't want to have sex, then don't. Period. If you do give into his invitations and you aren't sure of your choice, you may well regret it.

It's obvious that you care about him, and I know you want to make him happy. So, sit your guy down—with all clothing on and with plenty of space on the couch—and calmly explain your feelings. If he truly cares about you, then he will make the effort to restrain himself and his requests. Make sure you let him know how uncomfortable his comments make you feel. He may not even realize that this topic upsets you. He may have just got caught up in the moment and not understood how awkward this issue is for you.

> *The average teen boy doesn't wait out of a deep and abiding sense of respect. He waits because his girl sets a boundary.*

Just remember, no means no. Make sure you put yourself first and don't sacrifice what you want for a relationship.

Dr. Wes: Some guys may object, but Miranda is right on when she notes that all teenage boys want to have sex with the girls they are attracted to. It's the most natural of phenomena. However, wanting something does not make one entitled to it, and that's where our culture has shifted in the last few years, as far as teen romance is concerned.

Miranda echoes that quaint old saying intended to give girls more ways to say no: "If he really cares about you, he'll wait." Unfortunately, that was never true and it isn't now. The average teen boy doesn't wait out of a deep and abiding sense of respect for his partner. He waits because his girl sets a boundary. He then weighs the costs and benefits of accepting that limit and decides whether he wants to continue the relationship. This has gotten a lot tougher in the last ten years because, on the whole, girls are much more willing to hook up without the benefits of a relationship than they were in the past. So, a guy's options are more open now if he just wants to have sex. This changes his cost-benefit analysis, and from your perspective, undermines the boundary you've set. Whether he's a "nice" guy or a "bad" one, this still holds true and it puts you in an unfair competition with his other potential partners. Regardless of how he approaches you, that's the real source of the pressure you feel.

I strongly support your decision to remain abstinent, and encourage you to draw the line just as Miranda suggested—exactly where you think it should be. I hope your guy will weigh the benefits of being with you and decide it's worth it, even if it costs him the kind of sexual activity he desires. If he doesn't, you'll have to do your own analysis and consider the costs of keeping him around.

Take some time and think this through. You don't have to change who you are to become who he wants you to be, and the same is true for him.

Age Inappropriate

Dear Dr. Wes and John,

Will you please tell my seventeen-year-old, in print in front of everyone, that he or she (I don't even want to identify which) cannot date someone who is thirteen? My kid should be dating someone of the same age. Not only is it strange, it's against the law. My child won't listen to me, but I'll clip your article and stick it on the family bulletin board.

Dr. Wes: Happy to oblige. I've seen this many times over the years, typically an older guy and younger girl, but recently I've been seeing it the other way around. Either way, your child faces several problems and needs to get deadly serious about them in a hurry. First, it is unacceptable by any psychological estimate to be dating this way. Kids will argue that it's "only a four year difference" but there's no comparison between what you describe and, say, an eighteen-year-old and twenty-two-year-old dating. Seventeen-year-olds are at a completely different developmental level socially, sexually, and emotionally than thirteen-year-olds and should have no reason to see them as dating partners.

Likewise, there aren't any thirteen-year-olds ready to be involved with anyone outside of middle school.

The second problem is one of perception. Most older kids intuitively know what I've said to be true. If nothing else, they realize that others will look down on them for this practice. If your child needs John and I to reinforce something that seems obvious to everyone else, then he needs to see a good therapist because somewhere, something was lost in translation. Failing to accept basic social conventions is a common cognitive distortion among sex offenders. I'm not saying that's where your son or daughter is headed, but there is a distinct foundation here.

> *I'm talking about being arrested, charged with a sex offense, adjudicated, and placed in a detention facility for treatment.*

Finally, even if your teenager doesn't agree with me, John, the peer group, you, or society in general about this issue, then perhaps he or she should reflect on the fact that *it is illegal.* Of course, one has to actually engage in a sexual practice for the law to get involved, but many young people forget that this includes any sexual touching, fondling, oral sex, etc.

I'm not talking about a slap on the wrist here. I'm talking about being arrested, charged with a sex offense, adjudicated, and perhaps placed in a detention facility far from home for treatment and rehabilitation. I'm talking sex offender registry, up online where everyone can see your kid's picture and a map of where you live.

Parents need to teach kids of any age that sexual contact with a younger child is that serious. Too often, I've had a young teen in for evaluation and when asked what he thought would happen if he got caught fondling a seven or eight-year-old, he says he was afraid he'd be grounded. Failing to warn our children about the seriousness of this behavior just because we feel uncomfortable about the topic does them no service.

I commend you for trying and I hope this blunt advice helps.

John Murray: If your child were a celebrity, the tabloids would have humiliated him (or her) long ago. I don't mean to be rude, but when a seventeen-year-old hangs with a thirteen-year-old, he or she can't help but look like a sex offender. That impression permeates throughout the community, not just among friends and family, but potential employers and teachers writing recommendations. This relationship is on a one-way track to nowhere.

When it comes to dating, middle school and high school are separate realms that should never be mixed. A difference in age creates a difference in power. Your child can drive a car, take advanced courses, and go to R-rated movies. These powers, though relatively unimportant, can create a superhero image in the mind of the younger partner. If your child doesn't believe this, point to a twenty-one-year-old he or she admires.

Your child may object by saying, "I'm not doing anything illegal" because nothing sexual is occurring. But when questionable relationships turn sour, the younger party can easily play the sex abuse card and your kid's image will be damaged beyond repair, even if no legal action is taken. It doesn't matter what actually happened because it comes down to one's word against another's, and guess who is taken more seriously?

If your child doesn't have the courage to break up with this sweetheart, you ought to do the job. If your teen wants a dating partner, he or she should get a Facebook page, not a sevie.

Trying to Get Pregnant

Dear Dr. Wes and Marissa,

I have a friend who is barely seventeen-years-old and wants to have a baby. She has been with her current boyfriend for less than six months and says that she doesn't know whether she's completely in love with him or not, but she plans to get pregnant in August and graduate early in December, then move into a house with him. He's twenty-two and plans on supporting her with an income from a delivery job. My friend also says that she doesn't want her kids to grow up in a broken home like she had to. It seems to me that she selfishly wants to bring a baby into this world.

Marissa Ballard: Though it sounds like an odd situation, it is alarmingly common. The proof can be seen in local schools and by browsing online communities, including groups dedicated to supporting teenagers trying to become pregnant, websites advising and encouraging teenagers wanting a baby, and online forums for people to come together and talk about it.

Statistics say that the majority of teen girls trying to get pregnant come from divorced homes, and most had poor relationships with their parents. Victims of abuse are also more likely to become pregnant during their teenage years. My guess would be that she fits into one of these categories. Another reoccurring reason is wanting someone to love and to be loved in return. Yet, babies give very little love in the first years of their lives and require an astonishing amount of love and attention. I don't think your friend has an accurate view of what raising a baby will be like.

It's not about your friend. It's about the baby. The fact that this has not dawned on her tells us a lot about her readiness to be a mom.

Few teens are in a position to successfully raise a child and your comment about your friend's selfishness is right on the mark. Not only is having a baby at such a young age challenging, it's financially crippling.

Dr. Wes: Wow. This ranks near the top of the list of bad ideas. It's one thing when a young person has a birth control failure or isn't careful enough, but it's quite another when a couple intentionally set themselves on a course that all the research and clinical experience tell us is unwise. And yet, I see it often. As Marissa notes, teens in dysfunctional homes can become so desperate to feel what it's like to be in a "normal" family that they try to create one for themselves. However, those kids actually need to take more time, not less, to learn about themselves and others before trying to create the perfect family they missed out on as a child.

Finally, one can debate when kids are ready for sex, marriage, alcohol, driving, etc. But there's little debate as to whether teens are ready to have children. Brain development isn't complete until the early twenties when, among other things, young adults become a great deal less self-oriented and thus more capable of considering others first. Simply put: It's not about your friend. It's about the baby. The fact that this has not dawned on her tells us a lot about her readiness to be a mom.

It would be wrong, however, to end this discussion without noting the heroic effort of many young mothers. Despite staggering obstacles, many do the best job imaginable. However, while most love their little ones, they usually end up wishing they'd waited to experience the joys of parenting. Your friend will be no different. She should not deliberately put herself in such a position, just as she should not get into a car accident just because she sees paraplegics dealing heroically with their injuries. She has about fifteen to twenty years of reproductive opportunity at her disposal, plenty of time to grow up first.

Difficult Decision

Dear Dr. Wes and Julia,

My friend is fourteen and pregnant! She is asking me to help her decide whether to keep the baby or not. I don't want to tell her the wrong decision she will have to live with. What should she and I do?

Dr. Wes: I know how you feel. I remember having four pregnant teens on my caseload at the same time in the late 1990s. One was thirteen. That's the day I became a crusader on this issue, encouraging teens and their families to work together to prevent early pregnancy. I see at least one or two clients per week who are or have been affected by teen pregnancy, either their own or their parents'.

The difference, however, is that I am a therapist and you are not. I'm supposed to struggle alongside families and teenagers to address hard problems. You're only responsible to be a caring and supportive friend. It's unfair that you've been asked to share the burden of this decision. The best advice you can give your friend is for her and her family to connect with a therapist who can lay out all the options and help them reach a decision together.

You see, when we make a decision for ourselves, we make a decision for everyone. Early pregnancy doesn't just change a young girl's life; it impacts the father, her family, and the community. Too often, the baby's father becomes distant and unsupportive, and your friend will get little support from the state. Her best hope is family support, and as anyone who's done it will tell you, the dynamic of a parent parenting a parent is itself a reason to head to the therapist.

In addition to keeping the baby, I've seen teen pregnancies end in abortion and adoption, and there is no single option that fits every person. But there's one thing I can guarantee, every option creates potential for regret. Those who keep the baby will regret losing their teen years and young adulthood to the intense care a baby requires. Those who give up the child will wonder whether they should have kept it, longing for the day he or she might return to them as an adult. Those who choose abortion may wonder whether or not they made a wise or ethical decision, and they will face the judgment of others who believe they did not. A few people may reach a sense of peace about their response to an unplanned pregnancy, but I believe your friend, at fourteen, will have a difficult time becoming one of them.

Julia Davidson: Life would be a lot easier if there was a book called *I'm Pregnant...Now What?* that told you exactly what to do in a situation like this one. However, the choices associated with teen pregnancies are very subjective and, as Wes said, none of them are regret-free. In the end, it's your friend's call to make.

Even knowing all the factors—your friend's religious affiliation, whether or not the father is going to come through, her family's opinion or yours—would not bring you a step closer to selecting a perfect choice for her. Harsh as it is to say, she is on her own here.

I know you feel that if there was ever a moment to pull through for a friend, it would be now, but having you dictate her decision is definitely unfair to you. By asking you what she should do in a life-changing situation, she is demonstrating that she hasn't made any progress toward deciding for herself. She is rightfully scared and basically avoiding that fear by giving you a share of the responsibility.

Be as supportive as possible. Just letting her talk to you about what she feels could help her figure things out. Try to understand what she is going through—what many teens have gone or will go through.

Reader Response to
Pregnant Fourteen-Year-Old

Dear Dr. Wes and Julia,

I read your column every week and generally agree with your advice. However, I was a little upset with the advice you gave to a fourteen-year-old girl with a pregnant friend. I got pregnant at seventeen, and went through many of the same problems she will face. I considered adoption but knew I would always wonder whether it was the right decision. Abortion was never an option due to my beliefs. So, I kept my son. I agree wholeheartedly about the need for a great support system. I wouldn't have been as successful without my parents, even with the regular bickering between us. It's not easy and not many girls purposely get into it.

But almost everything you said was negative. There are a lot more resources for young parents than you let on. I graduated high school and am attending college and living on my own. I pay all my own bills and the only assistance I get from my parents now is babysitting. My son's father is not involved, but I have my son in activities where he's surrounded by good male role models. I'm glad you warned readers about the possible bad outcomes, but you should have mentioned some of the things that single and/or young mothers can still achieve, despite all the odds and obstacles.

Dr. Wes: We'd never want to upset a loyal reader who's come through an early pregnancy successfully, lives on her own, and is attending college. I have great respect for what you've done. While the difficulties you describe actually support the points we made, you remind us that many young moms do pull through. That wasn't the emphasis of our original column, which did read a bit like a horror story of teen pregnancy. In contrast, your letter brightened my day.

I don't agree, however, that many resources are available for teen moms. Instead, our society increasingly punishes them and their children. Government policy is now engineered to dissuade early pregnancy by withholding support, even though there is no correlation between the two issues. Most young moms succeed as you did, by their own wits, and in spite of limited resources, not because of them.

Your letter points out exactly what it takes to triumph in early pregnancy. First, one must actually make a decision and follow through on it, learning to desperately want the child, and making an affirmative choice to be a parent, regardless of the circumstances of conception. Otherwise, you're destined to parent halfheartedly, which is pretty hard to hide from your child. I commend you for that commitment.

Next, one must work constantly to balance caring for a child and getting one's own life in order. This is where the support system is vital because it allows a young mom to stay in school while providing a loving home. It's also where the party bus gets a flat tire. It's not that young parents can't have a good time. There's just little time left to do it when you're fully engaged in parenting, going to school, working, etc. Parenting is about sacrifice, something that isn't clear to young adults until they are, like you, in the throes of it.

Other factors that predict success for very young parents can't be easily changed. The family's financial situation, the parent's energy level, mental health, aptitude as a student, connection to the child's father, and raw tenacity (stick-to-it-ness) all improve the odds.

Julia Davidson: It is amazing to see how you've handled your situation, but, as Wes said, you're one of the exceptional ones who's been able to emotionally and mentally take on such a huge responsibility. Despite numerous sex-ed classes, talks with parents, and knowledge about all the details, most teenagers can't or won't wrap their minds around the idea of pregnancy until they come face-to-face with it. We focused on the negatives only to warn other teens in advance of what they might face.

Not everyone goes through every single trial and tribulation we described, and many do emerge as successful and proud parents. The advice I gave the fourteen-year-old and her friend reflected her age and the urgency of the letter. The emotional maturity and experience gained between the age of fourteen and seventeen is vast, and although yours is a shining example of what strong will and perseverance can achieve, I couldn't advise her as I would you.

It's important to deal with each situation singularly and hope that other teens learn from someone else's problem. Within that context, your story was a good balance to our advice, but not a replacement.

Icky STDs

Dr. Wes: When discussing sex, I've always said that the fastest way to shut down the neural pathways between a teenager's ears and his brain is to launch into a thoughtful lecture on the dangers of sexually transmitted diseases. If you throw in some icky pictures, you can actually increase the speed of that shutdown by a factor of three.

Unfortunately, Dear Teens, sexually transmitted diseases, especially HPV, herpes, and chlamydia, are on an epidemic rise with about 25% of sexually active teens contracting some form of STD in any given year. Why? Because, while teenage girls have generally mastered birth control, teens have yet to take seriously the likelihood of infection. If you think about it, this fits pretty well with what we know of your brain. You actually see peer pregnancy happening around you, so you can accept it's probability, and a short trip to the doctor can resolve those concerns.

However, all the birth control pills or Depo Provera shots on earth won't protect anyone from STDs. The Centers for Disease Control (CDC) note that chlamydia and gonorrhea remain the most common *curable* STDs among teens. While both respond to antibiotics, they can be tricky and sometimes go undetected, leading to more severe health consequences down the road. The CDC notes that it's not uncommon to see more than five percent of teen boys and five- to-ten percent of girls infected with chlamydia at any given time.

Properly used, condoms can limit exposure to chlamydia, HIV, and gonorrhea. But they're less effective for herpes and HPV, because they don't require any exchange of fluids, making them fairly easy to get via skin contact. And for those infections, there's no cure, only treatment.[5] About twenty-two percent of young adults have genital herpes (HSV-2), and its prevalence is increasing most rapidly among young white teens. The rate for twelve to nineteen-year-olds is now five times what it was just twenty years ago, and young adults age twenty to twenty-nine are now twice as likely to have HSV-2 as they were in 1986. The severity of cases varies dramatically from unnoticeable to very serious, so you want to do what you can to avoid becoming one of those statistics.

> *No one ever ends a story with, "...and then I got chlamydia and it sucked." I wish they would.*

Marissa Ballard: Quite a few people my age jump into sex at an early age and, by the time they graduate high school, have had more partners than they can count on one hand. We all hear about the good stuff that goes along with sex, but no one ever ends a story with, "...and then I got chlamydia and it sucked." I wish they would. The silence surrounding STDs helps increase their incidence.

While no one wants to discuss their sexual history with a new partner, teens need to step up and be mature about it. If you can't talk with a prospective partner about STDs, it's safe to say that you two should not have sex. Make sure to sit down and say exactly what you expect and what things you are okay with. Make an agreement and honor it.

---

[5] Vaccinations to prevent cancer-causing strains of HPV came to the market after this column ran, and we discuss them later. The other strains cannot be cured or prevented with medicine, but many go dormant after a few years.

That discussion is not only important for you, but for the other person as well.

Of course, the best way to stay disease-free is to be abstinent, but I am not naïve. So, my next suggestion would be to remain exclusively with one person. If you sleep with more than one partner, your risks will be higher, which will mean going to the doctor and having regular STD screenings. A lot of STDs don't have distinct symptoms, so even if you don't notice anything that seems problematic, it never hurts to make sure. All of the work that goes into getting tested may seem inconvenient, but it's a part of being sexually active.

Coming Out or Not?

Dear Dr. Wes and Samantha,

I'm a sixteen-year-old girl and my best girlfriend is really my girlfriend. We're together. But neither of our parents know this, and while only a couple of our closest friends know, they would never tell anyone. Our parents think we're just good friends and that we're inseparable. We've thought about this and we really love each other and we'd like to come out to our families, who are pretty cool about people being gay. But if we tell them, we won't be allowed to be together like we are now. We won't have any privacy and it will be just like if we were dating boys. We won't get to stay over at each other's houses and so on. What would you advise us to do?[6]

Samantha Schwartz: You and your girlfriend need to talk to your parents. Though you may enjoy the privacy you have right now, the longer you keep this a secret, the less respect you will get from your parents once you tell them. Coming out is a big step, but because they seem like open-minded people and you two seem ready, there's no time like the present to take it.

All teenagers, regardless of sexual orientation, face the decision of how to handle the physical aspect of a relationship. They have to balance the guidelines given by their parents, the influence of their friends, and their own personal views. Now you will, too.

---

[6] This question was not submitted by a reader, but was the on-site essay stem for Samantha's application. It won her the contest against strong competition. I added my side later that year.

You seem to be in a pretty serious relationship. When people fall in love, they don't want to hide their feelings. You shouldn't have to hide your attraction to your friend. However, you and your parents should talk about boundaries as you make this change. What are they comfortable with seeing? Can you hold hands in front of them? Can you give her a hug when she leaves?

And then there's the privacy issue. How much are they willing to give you? Having a sleepover with someone you are physically attracted to may be considered inappropriate by your parents. This is normal parental behavior and you'll have to be respectful of that. However, you could ask, for example, if you'll be allowed to watch a movie alone together downstairs while your parents are upstairs. This may be less intimate than you're used to now, but if you want to build trust, you have to make some concessions.

If you and your girlfriend can both sit down and have this mature talk with your parents, you'll strengthen your relationship because you will have jumped through this hurdle together.

Dr. Wes: To pretend that your g.f. is only a friend is so deceptive that it cannot help but land you in hot water down the road. If you were concerned that your parents wouldn't approve of your sexual orientation, I'd understand your reluctance to tell them. I could even support the decision not to come out. But what you're doing here is taking advantage of their naïveté by keeping your secret.

I'm sure you'll figure out ways around those limits, but you're just not playing on an even field by keeping this secret from them.

For example, if you drop the sleepovers, genuinely act as friends in the presence of your family, and carry on your private romance elsewhere, I'd say you are within your rights to privacy. But once you start gaining privileges and access to your girlfriend under false pretenses, you're acting unethically. You're also creating a situation where your parents will react badly when they eventually find out. You can't gain their support for any relationship that way.

You describe each family as being cool with the idea of being gay, which makes your choice in this situation even less cool. While parents have limited practical influence in these matters, they do have a right to advise you on your romantic life and to give you support. They also have a right to question your decisions and try and keep you within reasonable and healthy limits. They can't dictate your sexuality but they can set limits on where, when, and to some degree, how you practice it.

As Samantha notes, one of the most basic boundaries involves what you're allowed to do with romantic partners in the home. If you want your family to respect your sexuality, embrace your partner, and support you at this critical time of life, you have to also respect, embrace, and support their role and the limits they set. I'm sure you'll figure out ways around those limits, just as all teenagers do, but you're just not playing on an even field by keeping this secret from them.

Coming out can be complicated, frightening, exciting, and rewarding all in one. If you think your family will be open to you, the next step is obvious. If you prefer to keep things private for now, you'll have to come up with a more ethical approach than the one your using now.

Informed Consent

Dear Dr. Wes and Kelly,

There's no graceful way to say it, so I'm just going to be blunt; I am a transgendered individual. I started dating this great guy a couple months ago. We've been taking it really slow, only kissing and holding hands, but things are steaming up. The only thing is that I'm pre-operation, and my boyfriend doesn't know I'm transgendered. I haven't told him yet because he is from a conservative Christian background and I'm his first girlfriend. I'm worried that he won't accept me for who I am, and that I may scare him off completely. Please help me. Should I dump him to save him from the shock or tell him the truth about me and hope he'll want to continue our relationship?

Every relationship goes from where it starts, and this one has started badly.

Dr. Wes: I believe you are sincere in your desire to work this out so that no one gets hurt, and I'm certain you're going through tremendous agony over how to proceed. However, your decision to pursue this relationship without full disclosure is unethical. At this point, it's hard to imagine either scenario you propose leaving anyone's feelings and emotional health intact.

Over the years, we've discussed ethical conduct among gay and straight clients, adults and teens, guys and girls. So, this advice is not about your gender identity or sexual orientation. It's about honesty and integrity in human relationships. Withholding this key information from someone with whom you are becoming intimate is a blatant failure to afford your partner what we refer to as "informed consent"—the ability to make a decision about something with all the information at hand.

As a psychologist, I understand that you experience yourself as female and operate from that emotional and psychological perspective. While many readers will find that hard to accept, we'll save that for another day and focus instead on how your partner sees you. He has no idea that you're not physiologically male and you've not seen fit to share that fact with him. Doing so is frightening and you are quite likely to face rejection. But to avoid making a decision is to make a decision. In this case, you're not just making that decision for yourself, but for someone else too, while knowing full well that this relationship will alienate your partner from his family and faith, even if he were to accept you as you see yourself.

You've really placed yourself in a serious dilemma and I'd strongly encourage you pursue a therapy relationship to help sort out how you got here and how to avoid it in the future. Every relationship goes from where it starts, and this one has started badly. Your best bet is to either break it off and simply explain that you've had a change of heart, or break it off and tell him the truth in the process, along with the most serious of apologies. I don't know this guy, but I'm very concerned about your physical safety and his psychological health if you do share all. However, only you can decide which is the wisest choice. What you cannot do is continue to lie by omission.

Kelly Kelin[7]: When people come to me for relationship advice, I always feel as though I give everyone the same answer: be honest and communicate. The more I give it, the more I realize how quickly and simply that answer brings about change. If you wish to continue the relationship with this guy, then you obviously must tell him the truth. He will either accept you for who you are or things could go badly.

Wes is right. You should have been honest from the beginning. Wouldn't you expect the same level of candor from someone else? At some point early on there must have been a moment where you could

---

[7] Kelly changed her last name to Woods shortly after completing her tenure on Double Take. Her column byline remains Kelin, her name at the time they were written. She is however, listed as Kelly Woods for the authorship of this book.

have confided in him. I know this is a big bombshell to drop on someone, but honesty is essential. Even if you fear the outcome, it's better to be true to yourself.

I know this is a particularly hard decision to make, but the barriers that we face are opportunities for learning and growth. If this relationship ends, it won't be the end of the world. There is someone out there who will accept you for who you are.

If you decide to break it off without telling him why, you will never have that closure. Yet, as Wes says, telling could cause serious and perhaps dangerous consequences, so be careful. Either way, it's important to be true to yourself and others.

You shouldn't have to hide who you are.

Abstinence is Cool

Dear Dr. Wes and Samantha,

Your column talks a lot about kids deciding to have sex. What about if we've decided not to? Could you give some tips on how to be abstinent rather than just say that not very many teens are? My boyfriend and I already know that. We want to try anyway.

Dr. Wes: All you have to do is ask. I'm impressed that you've actually *made* a decision about this. Too many young people just fall into sexual activity or do it as a way of competing in a limited dating pool. Regardless of whether you're doing it for religious, health, or emotional reasons, remaining abstinent is a great choice.

The first tip I'd offer every teen who has yet to have sex is to sit down, think it through, and make an affirmative decision whether you want to do it, and let "no" be just as authentic a choice as "yes." If you're already sexually active, sit down and make a decision whether you want to continue to be. It's uncommon, but there's no reason you can't decide to let your sex life go dormant until you feel you're better prepared. This isn't like deciding between Wii and Xbox. It's a serious, consequential choice.

Next, precisely define what constitutes sexual activity versus abstinence. Will you kiss? Will there be touching? If so, where and how? Clothes on or off? If this seems too personal to discuss, then wait until you're mature enough to proceed. Be crystal clear about these limits with any partners early in the relationship. Of course, you'll lose some dating options, but you may well gain a sense of purpose in your sexual development.

Abstinence is one of those odd situations where you have to work harder to not do something than to do it. A healthy sexual appetite is a normal part of adolescence and young adulthood, so going against that is like standing up in a rushing river. You have to use a lot of energy to resist the current. To do so, you need other activities that involve healthy excitement and risk-taking. Fortunately, the idea that the world is so boring it demands we have sex is ridiculous. You can learn rock climbing or survival training. There are even places that allow you to race cars on a closed track. It's best if you can share those activities with your partner, allowing the two of you to build intimacy without having to end up violating your agreement.

The reactions of others can make you feel as though you're doing something wrong, like maybe you should be having sex.

Below, Sam offers one of the most honest and courageous commentaries on this topic we've seen over the years in the pages of Double Take.

Samantha Schwartz: I admit that my response to this is very personal, and something I wouldn't normally share. However, I can't answer your question with facts or statistics. I've been dating the same guy for nearly a year and ten months, and we are abstinent. We have chosen to wait at least until college—maybe longer. It's not a religious decision. We made it because we don't feel we're ready yet.

Because we've been exclusive for so long, people ask whether we've had sex and are often surprised when I say no. They ask whether he's pressured me. I explain that he agrees that we're not ready. I applaud you for also finding someone who not only respects your decision but also actually agrees with you.

The reactions of others can make you feel as though you're doing something wrong, like maybe you *should* be having sex. Instead of explaining why you don't, try just listening. You can probably think of a counterpoint for everything they say and that's fine, but keep your arguments to yourself. People who feel a need to argue with you about this may actually be questioning their own choice, needing to defend it to you and to themselves.

If outside pressure doesn't get to you, great! But, no matter how you and your boyfriend feel about abstinence, there is still pressure within your relationship to have sex. You're dating because you're attracted to each other, emotionally and physically. As Wes points out, it's human nature to want to express that and make the other person happy.

Having solid boundaries will allow you to make your behavior consistent with your values and beliefs. Separately decide what your limits are, then make a pact not to do anything that you have not verbally agreed to in advance. This way, you won't be questioning what you want while your hormones are going crazy. If you want to change those boundaries, that's fine, but talk about it first, and not in the heat of the moment.

Talking about sex (whether you're having it or not) can be pretty awkward. Stick to whatever you think is right for you and don't let others' opinions or vague boundaries keep you from sticking to your promise to each other and to yourself.

4 SUBSTANCE ABUSE

Mary Jane

Dear Dr. Wes and Kelly,

Marijuana has neither killed anyone (people kill people) nor been proven to be detrimental to your health, so why is it considered such a dangerous drug? Ancient tribes smoked the stuff as a means of peace with their enemies; it's been proven to greatly benefit cancer patients and even reduces male sperm count (population control!). Why is there such a negative stigma associated with it? And where did all these false "facts" come from?

Kelly Kelin: Since the fifth grade, we've been taught through various health classes and D.A.R.E programs that all drugs are bad for us and that we should not use them. We learned about drug abuse and what would happen if each drug was taken. For some students, this created fear. For others, curiosity.

To some, marijuana is bad because they classify it as a "gateway drug," leading to others like crack and heroin, even though this classification has no solid statistical proof. Others are certain that abusing marijuana will lead to a domino effect, damaging not only our general health but the economic and social aspect of society as well. There are some slight physical risks to marijuana use, including a higher heart rate and blood pressure, paranoia, and enhanced senses. Further, some marijuana contains the same cancer-causing compounds as tobacco. But many substances are branded with a warning label, including cigarettes and alcohol, which are legal.

The general perspective on marijuana is based on propaganda and emotion... but the propaganda goes both ways.

The positive attributes of marijuana include a wide range of clinical uses, including pain relief (particularly nerve damage), glaucoma, and movement disorders. It also increases appetite for patients who have disorders that diminish it.

Perhaps we need to start looking at things from a two-sided perspective. Yes, marijuana can be medically beneficial, and, yes, there are some factors and reactions to it that are bad. Yet, the laws restricting it should be loosened. Since 1973, Alaska, California, Colorado, Maine, Minnesota, Mississippi, Nebraska, Nevada, New York, North Carolina, Ohio, and Oregon have all enacted decriminalization laws. In some of those states, users no longer face jail time—not even arrest or criminal records—for the possession or use of small amounts of marijuana. Internationally, many states and nations have enacted similar policies.

Dr. Wes: Whatever we say in this column, many readers will not like it because as Kelly and our reader point out, the general perspective on marijuana is based on propaganda and emotion. Before the "pro-weed" readers light one up in my honor and the "anti-marijuana" readers light up the Internet in protest, let me add that the propaganda goes *both ways*.

Our reader joins the majority of his or her peer group, portraying weed as harmless and actually quite delightful. This is now the cultural zeitgeist among teens and young adults, even those who don't partake. Call me a 210-pound buzz kill, but I'll never be a fan of substance abuse. Sitting in this chair, I see one family after another whose marriages, careers, and families have been destroyed in the bottle or on the pipe, all of whom were quite sure that they were immune from addiction. And that doesn't touch the number who'll die this year from cigarette use, after enduring tobacco-related illnesses and consuming a large share of Medicare and other healthcare resources.

Of course, many folks use substances responsibly, and I see them too. But, on any given evening in this college town, I'd suggest you drive safely or not at all, because you're on the road with a bunch of people who have probably ingested some mind-altering substance and if they don't run into you first, they'll most likely get away with it.

I don't make any positive distinction between alcohol and marijuana. The research does suggest that pot is among the less physically addictive drugs. But a great many things are not physically addictive—like sex and *World of Warcraft*—each of which can press certain individuals beyond their capacity for control. Why would weed be any different? If it didn't modify perception, brain functioning, and response, then why would anyone spend money on it? As with anything pleasurable, some people are going to stop what they're doing and pay it more heed than other necessary aspects of life, often to their detriment.

And that's what we call an addiction.

Even if pot addicts are a minority, I've become increasingly frustrated with the absolute refusal by moderate to heavy users to see any negative impact on their own lives. Repeatedly, I've had young people tell me that they are lethargic, falling behind in school or work, inattentive, anxious, or even a bit paranoid. When asked how much they smoke, they become defensive and say, "That's got nothing to do with it!" The issue's off the table because the zeitgeist tells them that marijuana is good and anyone who says otherwise must also believe in evil fairies.

Kelly is correct. The propaganda on the other side isn't much better. Lumping marijuana in with harder drugs and suggesting that its abuse is worse than alcohol just isn't supported by the literature. Moreover, these scare tactics just make young people more willing to stick to their guns and ignore the possibility that all this smoking isn't such a great idea. They just laugh it off and check their calendars for the next 4/20.

Whether or not legalization is a worthy goal depends on your theory of what works and what doesn't. As a psychologist, I'd be a lot more excited about keeping marijuana illegal, if that actually did anything to reduce the rate of usage or interdict the supply. If anything, weed is easier for kids to get than alcohol and cigarettes because it is unregulated and underground.

Despite my general grumpiness about substance use—in fact because of it—I question whether our current approach to the "drug war" is getting teenagers, young adults, and society any closer to sensibility on this issue.

Drinking At Dances

Dear Dr. Wes and Marissa,

As you know, teenage drinking at school dances and activities has been a problem for a long time and is getting worse. What advice would you give to kids and parents about this issue, regarding safety and good decision making?

Dr. Wes: Before I go there, please let me preach just one little sermon. All the recent research is clear: Alcohol use during adolescence leads to long-term brain damage. This exceeds the impact alcohol has on adult brains for one simple reason—your brain isn't finished developing yet and won't be until at least age twenty-two. So, alcohol puts brain *development* at risk. The heavier the use, the greater the risk. This research is not politically motivated or government propaganda to get you to behave.

For most teens, however, keeping your brain fresh and healthy is not at the top of the list of fun stuff to consider, so these facts tend to go unnoticed. For parents, your committing brain damage should not translate into a twenty-four-hour vigil to avoid any contact with demon rum. It calls for exactly what you propose—some serious safety precautions and sensible decision-making.

I favor drinking-and-driving contracts where parents agree to bring you home in the event of your intoxication. This doesn't mean you get off without consequence. However, I recommend moderate punishment in such situations, versus *incredibly severe ones* when drunk driving is involved, like selling your car. And if calling in the rescue squad becomes a habit, your folks must consider stiffer measures.

As for "safe drinking" (and I use that term reluctantly), I'm alarmed when I hear party stories in which "Miss X" passed out and threw up nine times while everyone stood by and drunkenly did nothing except snap pix for Facebook. In such situations, you must consider alcohol poisoning, rather than assuming Miss X just needed to sleep it off.

Here are some signs to clip and stick in your wallet or save on the notes app in your phone:

- Miss X cannot be awakened.
- She has cold, clammy hands.

- She has unusually pale or bluish skin.
- Her breathing is slow or irregular, less than eight inhalations a minute, or ten seconds or more between any two breaths.
- She vomits while passed out and does not wake up during or after vomiting.

If any of these things happen, call 911 immediately. Do not worry about your precarious legal situation, except to know that it will get immeasurably worse if you don't act. Do not leave Miss X alone. Continue trying to revive her. Turn her on her side, so that if she does vomit she'll be less likely to choke on it. As lovely as that sounds, it's exactly how people die in these cases. If she stops breathing, perform CPR. If you don't know how, find someone who does. Hoping for the best won't save anyone.

So, how can a party full of wasted kids do any of these things? They probably can't. We've long suggested a "designated driver" as a way to keep people safe in the car. Some people at a party need to be designated as the Sober Patrol (catchy, huh?), and take care of everyone else.

An obvious suggestion would be for everyone to drink only in moderation. To often however, that one goes unheeded. So, it's important to know what to do when drinking gets out of hand.

Marissa Ballard: The rate of alcohol use among teens is enough to make you wish that prohibition had worked. One of the most important things you can do to protect yourself is to make sure that you're not riding to an event with someone who has intentions to drink, even if it's just a little bit. You never want to ride with someone who has, and you don't want to be left without a ride if they don't stay sober.

For some reason, the numerous public service announcements and school flyers are still not breaking through to students, and kids are still driving after they've been drinking or using drugs. No matter whether you feel capable of driving, if something bad happens and you hurt someone, you are going to be in a tough spot for a long time. Even if you only wreck a car you're bringing expensive and serious legal consequences upon yourself. Good luck explaining that one to your parents.

Apart from driving, if you're going to a be where alcohol is available, make sure that you bring someone along who is also not drinking. It's hard to be the sole person responsible for taking care of your drunken friends, but it's a worthwhile endeavor to ensure that they stay safe.

Besides, choosing not to drink will give you more pride than joining everyone else in the drunken festivities ever will.

Drink or Stay Home

Dr. Wes: In my early days as a family psychologist, I used to argue against the concept of peer pressure as a convenient excuse to blame someone else for your choices. The research backed me up, as most studies found that kids tended to make their own decisions on drug and alcohol use, and parent use predicted teen use-patterns far better than peer pressure.

As with everything else, I find that times have changed. In the last five to seven years, I've detected a real shift in how much the non-substance using crowd feels ostracized by the smokers and drinkers. I've heard a hundred versions of "My best friend says this is the year she's gonna smoke me up," or "Nobody's inviting me to parties anymore because I don't drink."

Everyone is expected to join in or stay home. This intolerance goes directly to the issue of free will.

We used to call sober people designated drivers, and they had probably driven everyone's car in school by graduation. But there seems to be less respect for that job these days and everyone is expected to join in or stay home.

This intolerance goes directly to the issue of free will. Drinking and smoking are decisions you get to make for yourself, and nobody else should have any vested interest in that choice. To judge a friend because they abstain, or worse to condemn them for it, is about as opposite of genuine friendship as anything I can imagine. Would anyone put up with an abstainer going around a party, getting up in your face, and launching into a long sermon on the evils of alcohol?

The same should hold true for those who prefer to enjoy their friends and social time without feeling obliged to party.

Miranda Davis: For many teens who don't drink, their friends still do. While you shouldn't alienate every friend who's ever been to a party, I'd caution you to avoid the ones who negatively affect your life. Look for friends that are similar in nature and whose character, values and morals align with your own. It's no secret that teenagers want to be accepted by their peers, but don't let that get you into a situation that you will regret.

While your friends' parents may not care that they drink, your parents could (and should) feel very differently. At the end of the day, you don't live your friends' lives and you're the only person who has to live with the consequences of your actions. Besides, all those Facebook pictures of you holding a beer may come back to haunt you someday.

If you choose not to drink, don't feel like you have to stand up and make an ordeal out of the situation. A simple excuse like sports practice the next day, "nosey parents," or having to get up early for work are all ways you can counter the pressure, without coming off as preachy or causing the more pushy partiers to judge you.

Your friends will continue to make their own choices, and all you can do is live your life the way you think you should.

Diet Pills

Dear Dr. Wes and Jenny,

My mom found my diet pills while going through my sock drawer a few weeks ago. She got really upset, so I decided to stop taking them, but now I'm really worried about gaining weight. Also, I don't have any energy and feel depressed. Should I try to talk to my mom about it, or just handle it myself?

Dr. Wes: Diet pills pose three problems: They don't work, are addictive, and can kill you, which is what we would call a no-win situation. Besides the fact that they're useless for long-term weight loss, they can raise your blood pressure, cause your heart to beat irregularly, and give you anxiety and insomnia. Once you're used to them, you may feel low without the kick of these drugs, most of which contain caffeine, now that ephedra is banned. However, diet pills are more likely to *increase* depression over time.

If you think you're depressed, it's better to find a good therapist to evaluate you, and if that doesn't do the trick, consider getting a referral for a medication consult. It's best for a mental health professional to closely chart your progress even if you do begin medication.

As for your weight, I've yet to meet a teenage girl who was happy with her body, as Jenny will point out below.

Jenny Kane: Why should any young woman be taking diet pills? There are many alternatives to losing weight, like going for walks every day or getting involved in a sport. Either activity will help you achieve your weight loss goals and will reduce the depression you've been experiencing. Exercise releases natural endorphins into your brain, which makes you feel happier. When most people take diet pills, their bodies get addicted to the substance, so when you quit your body goes through a withdrawal stage.

Your mother is probably upset that you feel the need to lose weight this way. She could also be disappointed because you didn't talk to her about your problems. So, talk to her about why you think you need to use diet pills. Your friends at school could also be a source of support. Don't be afraid to ask for help—there are many people out there, some you don't even know yet, who are ready to lend a hand.

Stimulant Abuse

Dear Dr. Wes and Marissa,

In your opinion, do college students abuse Adderall? Can this lead to more serious problems later on?

Dr. Wes: Absolutely, on both counts. And prescription drug abuse isn't just limited to college students or that particular medication. We see this problem in middle and high schools, and with Ritalin-type products as well. It's one reason clinics need to be very careful in writing these prescriptions for teens and young adults.

When our office prescribes any medication to teens, we have a frank talk with their parents about the potential for abuse or dependency. With college kids we have the same conversation, and try and stay vigilant about looking for signs of misuse. To understand the problem, one has to realize that these medications are stimulants, which, when abused, are more commonly known as "speed." They are similar to methamphetamine, though far less potent if taken orally, as they're supposed to be.

Reasons for stimulant abuse vary from the pseudo-sensible (using them to improve focus for studying or testing) to the dangerous (enjoying the high they create). Any reason is a bad one, however, because misuse can lead to significant health concerns and addiction. The only people who should be on these meds are those who have legitimate diagnoses of ADHD or other disorders, such as hypersomnia.

I've seen these meds do wonders for many young people and adults with ADHD. I've also seen folks misuse them with very negative consequences. For the non-ADHD crowd, they can cause anything from anxiety and sleeplessness to mania (extreme energy, excitement, or arousal), and even paranoia and full-blown psychosis. Physically, stimulant abuse can lead to heart problems and unhealthy weight loss. In people with a tendency toward bipolar disorder, the risks are even greater. This is why psychiatrists and nurse practitioners usually start patients on low doses in order to be sure they don't make things worse rather than better.

A major allure of stimulants for teens is that they do help one focus their attention, stay up later, and get more work done. That sounds great until you realize that over a fairly short period of time, people build tolerance to the drug, meaning you need more and more of it to achieve the level of response you experienced when you first took it.

Prescription pills are more enticing because they're easy to conceal.

The other interesting thing about stimulants and studying is that you don't always turn out as good a product as you think. This is because the heightened arousal these drugs create can make you feel grandiose. I recall one of my teachers sharing that she'd used amphetamines before a big oral exam in college. On the very first question she recalled presenting the material brilliantly, offering amazing insight about which her professors would surely be talking for years to come. When she finished, the lead professor turned to her and said, "That's all very nice, Ms. Jones, but what did it have to do with the question?"

She flunked the exam.

So, if you're asking this question because you have abused or want to abuse stimulants, I'd suggest an immediate change of course.

Marissa Ballard: When I was in junior high, three of my friends got in trouble for sharing their Adderall. The problem with kids using pills has only gotten worse since then. Anyone can be misusing this type of medication—the person with straight A's and the one who is flunking all of his classes.

I know people who hardly ever come to school without having taken something. I've been offered dozens of different kinds of pills myself. Some people are just "generous." Others are looking to sell them for a profit. When I had my wisdom teeth removed, people were asking if they could buy the hydrocodone I had been prescribed for the pain.

Prescription pills are more enticing than any other drug because they're easy to conceal. It's often impossible to tell whether or not a person has taken them because there's no scent, no bloodshot eyes—nothing. Because it's so easy to get away with using them, teenagers do not take the repercussions seriously. Sure, it's fun now, but what about when you go off to college, or get a job? How long before it really messes up your life and your ambitions?

Our schools do not take the issue of drug abuse as seriously as they should. Such dangerous drug use goes on every day and no one seems to notice. Know that the total number of students who report taking prescription drugs on surveys plus the number of students who are caught is significantly lower than the actual number of students who are taking prescription pills. We need to start taking this issue more seriously or else it will only get much worse.

eBay Addiction

Dear Dr. Wes and John,

I'm in high school and I love to buy things on eBay—be it a purse or a CD or a shirt. The problem is that what started out as an occasional purchase here and there has turned into an obsession. I love bidding and I'll keep raising my bid, and then as soon as I win, I'm overcome with this sick feeling. In the past month, I've spent way more than I can afford. Should I ask my parents to bail me out? Or should I not even tell them? I haven't heard of anyone else with this problem. Is it common?

Dr. Wes: Tis the season to shop 'til you drop and, apparently, the eBay craze is not limited to adults. I am intimately familiar with eBay myself. It has a particular allure because it combines a number of pleasures. It has a fun competitive flavor like the old country auctions that I attended as a kid, the immediacy and convenience of online purchasing, and best of all, the mindboggling scope of the worldwide web. I admit it's the first place I go to look for tools, hobby items, and clothes. I even purchased my entire office computer network system on eBay and got terrific deals in the process.

In fact, eBay is a fine example of how good things can become extremely problematic before you know it. You'll notice that no one becomes addicted to boring, marginal things, which goes against the very brain chemistry of addiction. Almost to a fault, what is interesting stimulates your brain in such a way as to encourage overuse, obsession, and addiction. Worst of all, you only need a bank account to use PayPal, so you can forgo the usual requirement of a credit card to make purchases.

So, what to do? I'm willing to bet that eBay is not going to get less interesting for you over time. It's every-changing, growing, and expanding. So, you probably need to figure out how to restrain yourself. Set a budget for items each week or month, and limit yourself to that and only that. Try to restrict your purchases to practical things you really need—clothes, shoes, etc. That way you get all the fun and bargains and a lot less useless junk. If you're already in debt, however, you'd better resign your account now until you get caught up. You might also want to let the folks help you with this. Be honest with them and let them know you're having problems limiting yourself. Work up a bailout scheme which also allows them to put some limits on your spending, if you can't do it yourself. If none of this works, John offers some more extreme measures for your consideration.

Gotta go. I'm tracking the bids on a really cool drywall tool, and the auction closes in a few minutes.

John Murray: Unfortunately, compulsive shopping is very common in our society. On both an individual and national level, we are endangering our economic security by spending more than we can afford. The root causes of compulsive shopping are similar to the causes of other addictions: We have a feeling of emptiness and low self-esteem, for which we try to compensate with a behavior whose indulgence gives us a temporary high, followed by feelings of defeat and powerlessness, which only starts the cycle again.

Fortunately, however, the twelve steps for overcoming addiction were laid out in 1939 by Bob Smith and Bill Wilson, founders of Alcoholics Anonymous. Its success has generated many spin-offs, including Debtors Anonymous. You would do well to read the steps yourself, but here's a short take. The first involves analyzing your character and asking a higher power to remove the defects from it. It's good that you've admitted you have a problem, but now you need to look at the root causes. Are you worried about school, or stressed about family life? Examine yourself honestly and ask what holes you are trying to fill with shopping. Once you've identified your problem areas, humbly ask your higher power to remove those shortcomings.

Now comes the hard part—making amends. It sounds drastic, but I agree with Wes. Tell your parents the whole story, then ask them to suspend your account. This sounds like admitting defeat, but it's actually an important step toward your victory over compulsive shopping. A couple months without it will give you time to find other interests and to put your priorities in perspective. Your parents probably won't foot the bill, but they should admire your proactive response. You might also want to find a constructive hobby or some other distraction from eBay.

Finally, for twenty minutes each day, ask your higher power for the serenity to accept what you cannot change, the courage to change what you can, and the wisdom to know the difference. This last step is not a personal suggestion, but a time-tested formula that has helped millions recover from addiction.

Will you be next?

5 MENTAL HEALTH

Me, My Boyfriend and My Anxiety

Dear Dr. Wes and Julia,

I have always suffered with anxiety-driven depression. My boyfriend hasn't. He doesn't understand how to cope with this. How can I make him understand?

Julia Davidson: Being frustrated with your boyfriend is understandable; it seems insensitive or lazy not to make an effort to understand a loved one's issues. However, your frustration mixed with his confusion only weakens your relationship and causes a rift in communication. Instead, try to calmly teach him about your situation. You might explain how your depression and anxiety come about, how it makes you feel, how it might affect family members or loved ones, and maybe reference someone else who has it. If you keep the conversation positive and in favor of his being informed, he may see that your relationship can benefit from more understanding.

Your guy may feel as though he's always moving from one emotional incident to another.

Try to be forgiving if he doesn't fully get it at first. It's biologically typical for girls to want an emotional connection and for guys to want a physical one. Each has to understand this about the other. Make sure he knows how much his caring and understanding mean to both of you and that your relationship is valuable enough to try and work things out.

If you try this sort of nonaggressive approach and he still doesn't get it, you might reconsider how well you're matched. You don't benefit from the extra anxiety and he doesn't benefit from feeling like your relationship is unsatisfactory. Both of you should keep your personal needs at the forefront of your thinking. If those needs aren't met, it's probably better to separate as friends.

Dr. Wes: Parents and professionals don't always realize the importance of processing and understanding romantic relationships in adolescence, or see them as worthy of intervention. Unfortunately, few teen relationship issues are as difficult to address as a partner's mental health. At this age, most boy- or girlfriends simply aren't emotionally equipped to handle someone else's anxiety or depression. So, the advice a therapist offers you and what another therapist will tell your boyfriend are likely to be very different things. It's worth addressing both sides of that issue to do justice to your question.

As Julia notes, you should help your boyfriend understand your issues and how they may influence your behavior, emotional display, what you say, and how you interact. Your guy will need to realize how displays of anger or irritability are actually anxiety-driven. He may feel as though he's always moving from one emotional incident to another, and he'll have to learn with great precision what to take personally and what not to. None of this sounds any easier than it is, especially for teenagers.

Unfortunately for you, the standard advice to your boyfriend will be to think very carefully about how involved he wants to get with you. Our culture deeply cherishes the "love conquers all" philosophy, despite a lot of research that suggests otherwise. Instead, what you have to do to maintain this or any relationship is also serious and difficult. By working with a therapist and perhaps a prescriber, you can learn about how your anxiety affects your approach to relationships, how you define and understand reality, and how you assign meaning to what others do, all of which guides the way in which you respond to your world.

A big part of how any relationship goes for you will involve how you let yourself trust and how you attempt to enforce trust in your partner. This is where the anxious folks struggle, as they can at times, become rather controlling. So, it's not really enough to want to cope with your diagnosis. You really have to be on top of it, and until you are, it's too much to expect any romantic partner to be.

If all the parents are okay with it, I'd suggest bringing your b.f. to a therapy session to help you educate him and vice versa. If he's still not able to be helpful, I agree with Julia—you really have to question the value of the relationship at this point in your life. I realize that is itself an unnerving idea, but it's also necessary.

The path to love is long, and rarely simple and straightforward, especially when you're struggling with your own psychology along the way.

Diet and Mood

Dear Dr. Wes and John,

Does dieting affect your mood? If so, which diets are better than others?

Dr. Wes: Diets and dieting do affect your moods for good or ill. I found a good analogy by clinical nutritionist Samantha Heller, MS, RD, who suggests the relationship is kind of like a chemistry set. She notes, "If you are chemically balanced your moods will be balanced." This is a bit of an oversimplification because a lot of other things affect one's mood—namely, environment, exposure to trauma, and heredity. However, people with low risk for depression or anxiety can create mood problems by eating in certain ways. Those at higher risk can make things much better, or worse, by how they eat. In one example, researchers found that intake of sugar, caffeine, alcohol, and chocolate had a negative influence on mood, while increased water intake, vegetables, fruit, and oil-rich fish had a positive effect. No surprises there at all.

As you've probably gathered from media coverage, sugar and certain carbohydrates that turn into sugar quickly are by far the biggest offenders. These include just about everything that's fun to eat—cookies, cakes, pies, pancakes, potato chips, pop, and even fruit juices. Just writing this makes me hungry.

These foods, which Americans consume by the truckload, cause your body to respond with a big shot of insulin. Many repetitions of this sugar alert/insulin cycle cause your body to become less and less efficient, leaving you at risk for diabetes and other problems. It also affects your mood, creating a down state once the sugar high wears off.

On the other side of that equation, if you don't eat enough carbs during the day your blood sugars will tank, leaving you with a blah feeling that may be mistaken for depression. This is one of several problem dieters experience as they starve their bodies, then rebound and eat too much, then feel guilty and go back to starving.

I'm not a nutritionist, but I would strongly urge you to begin any diet only under the supervision of someone who is well-versed in teen nutrition. I will say that one big "non-secret" of dieting for mood stability is to eat smaller meals more frequently so you can keep your blood sugar stable. You should also look into the benefits of fish and fish oils. There's mounting scientific evidence that folks in fish eating countries have better mental and cardiac health. I'll leave it to you and your physician to determine whether these suggestions apply to you, but they've been helpful for others.

The other factor in mood management is, of course, exercise. It's a clear medical fact that exercise helps improve mood stability, energy, and psychological coping resources. One doesn't have to run cross-country to get those benefits. A regular walk, jog, or other physical activity should get the job done.

John Murray: Sudden changes in eating habits can also throw your body off-kilter. When you eat the same types of food every day, your body adjusts to make the most efficient use of them and comes to expect them every day. If you usually drink a Coke at lunch, you likely feel a Coke craving right before noon. When switching to a healthier diet, you're denying your body the toxins it has become so used to, so expect some resistance.

The good news is that once you stick to a healthy diet it becomes easier to avoid unhealthy foods. Just make sure the one you choose is sustainable. Don't starve yourself on a fad diet, because, as Wes points out, you'll immediately gain the weight back once you come off it. Clinical studies have shown yo-yo weight patterns to be worse for the body than obesity.

When talking about mood and dieting, distinguish between real hunger and "head hunger." Real hunger is the burning or growling you feel in your stomach. Head hunger is the desire to eat food because you're upset. It's natural to be stressed, but make sure you relieve this stress in healthy ways, like exercise, rather than trying to eat your feelings away. Your body wasn't built to binge on fat or sugar, and doing so will only aggravate your mood swings. Eat only when you are hungry and never when you're angry, tired, or lonely.

Americans like to develop patterns around eating, but it's okay to be countercultural. Not every wonderful meal needs a dessert. If you're already full, you don't *have to* finish your meal. On major holidays like Thanksgiving, don't feel you need to gorge in order to spread the holiday cheer. There will be plenty of leftovers on Friday.

In the end, effective dieting comes down to mood and whether you can keep your head in the midst of your passion.

Self-Harm

Dear Dr. Wes and Marissa,

My friend and I were fighting yesterday online. Then we both came to our senses, said sorry, and expressed our true feelings. But since last week, she keeps thinking of doing bad things to herself because she thinks she's disappointing everyone. She has an X on her waist and hand. She's not cutting exactly—she uses a needle and gently scrapes it against her skin until it's like someone scratched her in the shape of an X. I haven't talked to her since yesterday, but she said she might need help. I am worried about her.

Dr. Wes: It's not clear whether you think your argument provoked the cutting or the relationship has been strained because she became self-harmful. Either way, you are not responsible for her behavior.

Broadly speaking, cutting teens can be divided into two groups and it's important to understand into which one your friend falls. The first are similar to anorexics in that they tend to be "repressors," bottling up their problems and taking them out on themselves. Their families tend to have high expectations, which the cutter feels he or she can't meet.

Beating around the bush won't do you any good. You'll have to be blunt.

Sometimes that's accurate, and other times the teen is just insecure, but either way the cutter feels they don't measure up. Your friend hints at this when she worries about "disappointing everyone."

Cutters deal poorly with conflict at home or at school, preferring to avoid upsetting anyone, instead turning their anger and angst inward. More often than not, they're seen as "perfect children," easy to get along with, mild-tempered, obedient—all the things parents adore in their children. That does not mean cutters are well-adjusted. Instead, they simply hide their pain. In fact, one of the principal goals in treating cutters is helping them be more like normal teens, expressing their mood swings, showing anger, and getting into conflict. That's hard for families to take, but it helps the cutter find a better way to deal with the struggles of growing up. Fortunately, cutters are no more likely to commit suicide than anyone else. The bad news is that the lifelong scarring becomes an unfortunate reminder of all the pain the teen was trying to get rid of in the first place.

The second group includes those who get into cutting because their friends do it, or they want to gain the attention of family or peers. These kids are even harder to treat because they're acting out, not turning inward. They will persist long after the other kids have found a resolution and moved on. They're actually kind of rebellious when compared to the first group, tending to cut in very obvious places and to do so in the company of others.

Of course, kids can get started in one group and end up in the other, so these categories are just a way to understand the basic issues. In either case, encourage your friend to go to therapy as an important first step. You could even offer to go with her, as many cutters are reluctant to seek help alone.

Marissa Ballard: Cutting became pretty common among a group of people I knew when I was in junior high and I saw both of the categories that Wes describes. The ones who just did it for attention were the hardest to sympathize with. They would barely scratch themselves and then parade it around like some badge of honor. It seemed almost like an epidemic, but from what I can tell, it was something that most of my friends were able to stop with help.

What you need to do depends on how severe you think the situation is. If I were you, I'd first try to convince her to talk to her parents, who can help her find someone to talk to. Cutting can become very addictive. From what you have said, it doesn't sound like it's that serious yet, but stopping it early is important. I really think it's in her best interest that you say something. I've confronted a few of my friends head on, and let me tell you right now, it's not easy. Not by a long shot. Beating around the bush won't do you any good. You'll have to be blunt.

As Wes said, the worst thing about self-mutilation is the lifelong scars that it can leave behind. Since she's doing minor damage so far, it's an ideal time to point out these cosmetic ramifications. I don't think any teenage girl wants to knowingly put big gnarly scars on her body for the whole world to see, but if the vanity angle won't work, try something else.

You don't have to play the savior here, taking responsibility for what she does. Just be a friend, be there for her, and try to give her support.

Finding a Therapist

Dear Dr. Wes and Jenny,

I saw your column on cutting.[8] My cousin is in trouble. She's tried therapy and medication, but she continues to struggle with depression, substance abuse, and self-mutilation. Recently, she injured herself at school and the nurse had to call her mom to come get her. How can my cousin find something that works?

Dr. Wes: Your cousin has a classic cluster of problems. Helping her will require a heroic effort from her family. It frustrates me to hear that her mom has tried to involve her in therapy and med management and something has failed, because I'm a big advocate of that approach.

Our job as caring adults is to help kids make it to adulthood with as few scars, real and meta-phorical, as possible.

However, mother and daughter need to understand that not all treatment is created equal. Success depends on two things: the client and the professional. I strongly suggest they try again (and again) until something works. Here are my therapy-search guidelines for tough situations.

- **Find a good match.** Kids need therapists who capture their attention and win their hearts. There has to be a connection and therapy has to be influential. If your cousin is not a big talker, the last thing she needs is a therapist who sits in silence and waits for her to speak, and some do exactly that. A skilled therapist knows how to "feel" her way through a session with a qui-

---

[8] This column is found under the heading "Cutting" in Chapter 5 of *Dear Dr. Wes...Real Life Advice for Parents of Teens.*

et kid. If after two or three sessions there's no connection, move on.

- **Look for trained professionals who work with teens.** It is perfectly appropriate to ask about this before your first session and most therapists should provide you with a résumé on request.

- **Look for in-house medication management.** Medication appointments for your cousin need to be very frequent, not once every ninety-days for ten minutes.

- **Involve Parents.** In difficult cases, teens should not routinely be seen in therapy without ongoing consultation with their parents. This *does not* mean the therapist downloads to the parents everything the kid says. It means the therapist advises the parents on how to work better with their son or daughter.

- **Leave with specific strategies.** Some therapies can drift and, in many cases, that's a great journey of discovery. But a therapist for a case like your cousin's cannot simply offer a caring ear. He or she has to facilitate problem-solving, too. A skilled therapist will be "kindly blunt" in order to get to the heart of the matter.

- **Give it Time.** As much as parents and insurance companies hate to hear it, the problems your cousin presents do not go away quickly. When the right therapy is found, the family has to stick with it. The ultimate healing for adolescence is growing up. Our job as caring adults is to help kids make it to adulthood with as few scars, real and metaphorical, as possible.

Jenny Kane: Medication isn't always the best option for everyone, and some teenagers do not feel like opening up to a therapist, either because they're afraid what they say will get back to family members or that they just don't believe it will help. If either of these scenarios is the case, then help your friend overcome her preconceived notions of therapists and encourage her to try again. To show your support, you can even offer to go with her and be a part of the family sessions.

Also, when you're talking to your cousin, ask if she will promise to stop and call you or another person close to her whenever she feels like hurting herself. The best thing you can do is be there for her. Make her aware that people really care about her and that it hurts you to see her hurting.

Confidentiality in Therapy

Dear Dr. Wes and John,

If a young man was using illegal drugs and asked a therapist for help, would the therapist have to report it to the police?

Dr. Wes: An excellent question, and one that many kids wonder about. It's not just an issue of drugs, but any conduct that a person wants to discuss in therapy, but doesn't really want to have shared with authority figures. The answer revolves around client-therapist confidentiality, which we take very seriously.

First, let's address the easier question—do therapists have to report drug use or other illegal behavior to the police. The answer is no. In fact, it is a violation of any client's confidentiality to contact the authorities unless the therapist believes that the client is going to do serious harm to someone or has committed child abuse. Beyond this, therapy must be based on the assumption that a client should be able to share information freely and in confidence.

Courts occasionally order therapists to testify about a client or release their records. If a court tried to subpoena your records, however, you would ask your attorney to "invoke privileged communication" in objecting to their release. If you have court involvement of any kind or you are in foster care, you must talk with your therapist about any other limits on confidentiality.

Generally, what is shared with your parents is up to you as long as the therapist and your parents agree on that up front.

Disclosures to parents present a more complex situation. The short answer here is that most therapists understand the need for confidentiality among teenagers, but they must balance this against the young person's best interests. Thus, most therapists try to maintain strict limits on what they're willing to divulge to parents, which they should discuss during the first session with you and your folks. If a therapist doesn't make this completely clear, just ask.

Generally, what is shared with your parents is up to you *as long as the therapist and your parents agree on that up front.* Rarely, maybe two or three times in my career, a parent will refuse to allow treatment if the teenager's records are to be kept confidential. Usually, these cases involve legally complicated, high-conflict divorces. Many of us won't agree to work with a family under those circumstances, because no teenager is going to open up if the therapist is going to take it straight back to her folks, which would make therapy pretty much pointless.

On the other hand, if a therapist believes that a teenager is or might begin doing something extremely harmful to himself or someone else, we're obligated to break confidentiality. It's very important to find this out before you say something that crosses the line.

Finally, a family oriented therapist must balance privacy with good and honest family communication, so we may at times encourage a teen to share troubling thoughts and feelings with family members.

Other than those exceptions, My policy is to never share information about a teenager without his permission.

John Murray: We all have closet skeletons we'd rather not discuss, but honesty is essential when discussing problems with a therapist. Don't worry about what he'll think of you. Therapists have heard every one in the book and they're paid to help, not judge you. But it's difficult for a therapist to offer solutions if you can't tell him the whole problem. For example, if you're taking a narcotic, you might notice its effects on your mood, but if your therapist doesn't know about this, she might incorrectly diagnose you with a psychological disorder.

Your physician also needs to know about any illegal drugs you take, because they can interfere with other medications, sometimes with deadly effects. Conversations with medical personnel are usually protected by doctor-patient privilege as well, but you might want to ask about the law and their policies on this matter.

The risk of being reported pales in comparison to the risk of facing a drug problem alone. Counselors and psychiatrists can assist in breaking the addiction cycle, but only if you ask first and are honest about your problems.

Depressed Boyfriend

Dear Dr. Wes and John,

When you love a guy with some "issues" like depression, how can you help him crack his shell?

Dr. Wes: The first thing to remember above all else is to not let his depression become yours. Psychological problems can be kind of infectious among dating partners, as depressed kids find each other and become a sort of mutual support system. That sounds great, and sometimes it is. However, two sad, dark, reclusive teens can often drag each other down rather than lift each other up. So, ask yourself whether you're attracted to this guy because he seems so much like you. If so, then you may be at some risk of making things worse for yourself and for him.

If instead you see yourself as very different from your boyfriend, ask yourself whether you're attracted to him in a sort of client-therapist way. I especially worry about you wanting to "crack his shell." Many young people really like dating someone who *needs* them and depressed partners are very needy. That's really gratifying and romantic…until it's not. Teenagers aren't designed to be therapists and dealing with a depressed partner can overwhelm even an emotionally strong teen. Your reach on this may exceed your grasp, which leads us to something that may really help.

Therapy is where any shell-cracking should take place. If he's already seeing someone, ask your guy and/or his family if you can come for a session or two. If this is a fairly serious relationship the therapist should be interested in getting your perspective on things, and may be able to troubleshoot situations with the boyfriend before they become worse. You can even learn communication and new ways of relating that support his recovery. Relation-

As a sixteen-year old, you aren't entirely responsible for your own life, much less your boyfriend's.

ships are very important for teenagers—depressed or not. I always welcome family, school and community support of a client's wellbeing.

Depending on how your boyfriend expresses his depression, you can also help by just listening, taking him out so he doesn't isolate himself, or suggesting alternatives to self-destructive behavior. While accepting his views of school, family, friends, etc., you may also suggest less negative ways of thinking. This may be a little annoying to him at times, but if you're careful not to sound like Little Miss Sunshine, he'll realize that in many ways depression isn't just about how the world really is, but how we think about it.

And finally, always, always, ALWAYS share serious concerns about suicide with his therapist or loved ones. I know ratting out one's boyfriend is not socially acceptable and might even put the relationship at risk, but if you have any reason to worry, you have no other ethical choice.

John Murray: Your response will ultimately depend on what type of depressed person your boyfriend is. While some try to work out their problems by sharing them with their peers, others act like psychological parasites who simply try to make others feel their pain. Which one of these he is should be revealed by your dialogue.

Listening to upset people is good advice, but as Wes said, it only works if he's trying to pull himself up. It sounds strange, but some people actually enjoy making themselves depressed, and letting others know it. I've been there. Does your boyfriend try to interrupt your stories? If you express concerns about your classes and he goes into a tirade about why *his* classes are so difficult, he's begging for attention. If he's constantly shifting the subject to his problems and trying to make yours pale in comparison, listening may not help. On the other hand, if your boyfriend is genuinely interested in helping himself, an understanding ear could help him sort things out.

Try and engage him in some interesting activities with you. While dating someone, it's easy to get into the dinner and DVD rut, but passive activities won't help your boyfriend much. Try playing sports or even a board game together with friends, and you might be surprised at the results. This forces your boyfriend to do things rather than have things happen to him, which is the first step to overcoming depression. It's easier to take control of your life if you know you can control your chess pieces. The other benefit is that taking control of his situation will release a healthy pleasure in his brain, which may have a ripple effect in changing his view of things. Instead of passively hanging out, tell your boyfriend it's time to have fun—whether he likes it or not.

Just remember, some shells you can't crack. As a sixteen-year old, you aren't entirely responsible for your own life, much less your boyfriend's. If his attitude becomes self-destructive, tell him, "I care for you very much, but you need better help than I know how to give."

Self-Esteem?

Dear Dr. Wes and Julia,

Everything I read talks about self-esteem and being true to yourself. Is that something that comes with age, because I don't know anyone at school who feels good about themselves? I'm finding out that people I thought had it "all together" hate themselves too.

Dr. Wes: Self-esteem seems like such a good concept. We *should* experience positive feelings, confidence in our physical, mental, and emotional attributes, and take pride in our achievements. Logically, those who see themselves in a more positive light will have fewer problems.

Unfortunately, like so many good ideas, this one's gotten a big work-over by pop psychology, making it into the magic cure-all for every teen problem. If you struggle with mental health, drug use, body image, sexuality, bullying, schoolwork, etc., then the default diagnosis is low self-esteem and the prescription is to get more.

Sounds too easy, doesn't it?

Your question belies the problem to the solution of self-esteem. When it's treated like a commodity to be gained or lost, it becomes another reason to feel bad about yourself, because somehow you're missing something that everyone else supposedly has. As you point out, we don't really have a large sample of good self-esteem teens out there to judge by, so for all we know "low self-esteem" is the norm and "high self-esteem" a lofty goal. Like you, I find that no matter how cute, funny, athletic, interesting, or intelligent they may be, many teens are in a constant battle with both the real and the metaphorical mirror.

I think self-esteem is less about a personal state of being than it is about a social presentation.

Maturity may help your self-esteem, but I'd lean more toward the change in social environment that occurs in late adolescence. Self-reflection comes from advanced abstract thinking, so before age ten or eleven, we aren't really evaluating ourselves that way. As teens, self-esteem emerges from who we interact with, and how they perceive and treat us. This is why some kids do great until sixth or seventh grade, then suddenly become full of self-loathing. Their relationship to the environment changes dramatically, just as they become more able to consider it with intensity. So, the best remedy for low self-esteem is to be sure your life after high school puts you in healthy and positive environments.

All-in-all, I prefer to focus on "self-hope," the idea that one has a vision for herself and a sense of how to get there. This is easier and more practical to teach kids than a vague and illusive notion of "feeling good about myself." Take a look at who you want to be and make a list of those attributes, goals, hopes, and dreams. Let someone—a parent, sensible friend, counselor—review your list for a reality check. Then figure out the steps to getting there. This can be as small as getting a 3.5 GPA next semester, or as large as getting into the college you want. It could be a healthy diet, more exercise, or a post-graduation road trip. It matters less what the goal is than the fact that you develop your ability to achieve it. The more you do this, the more you'll respect yourself and your abilities. While this may garner the admiration of others and thus raise your self-esteem, your own personal successes will make you far less dependent on the fleeting commodity of other people's approval.

Julia Davidson: Like most teenagers, I've had too much experience with this topic. In seventh grade my self-esteem was nearly nonexistent. Eighth through tenth grade was spent seeking, learning, and developing it. Now that I finally have "self-esteem" it feels useless and excessive. Having it seems fabricated or overdeveloped.

I think self-esteem is less about a personal state of being than it is about a social presentation. If you're honest with yourself, how you feel and how you present yourself are two different views of the same person. The way someone presents herself to peers may take adjusting, as a normally quiet person becomes more bubbly and outgoing.

It's pretty obvious in school that everyone seeks a desperate balance between individuality (who they truly are) and acceptance (what everyone wants them to be). It's easier and more fun to fit in. You tell a joke or make a comment and bam, you're accepted. By relying on this version of yourself, you build self-esteem for something that is either partially or not at all a real piece of you.

Then, when people get older and start to rethink those personas, issues such as self-esteem play a large role. Rejecting peer acceptance means having to build up a different kind of self-esteem, make some new friends, accept feelings you didn't know you had, and so on. It's tough, and anyone who feels that pull between rejection and acceptance might "hate themselves," not for their lack of real self-esteem, but for the rejection of their social identity.

Regardless of how many extra personality traits you portray or believe are real, there's always a genuine person inside. Only there do you—not the situation or people surrounding you—feel most comfortable. Having that honest *self*-esteem to fall back on is what gives people the quality of being true to themselves.

Anger Management

Dear Dr. Wes and John,

I need help with my anger. I am going to a therapist. What else can I do?

Dr. Wes: Since you're already seeing a therapist, we'll suggest some strategies drawn from "cognitive behavioral therapy" to help that process along.

Focus first on your "self-talk," the stuff you say to yourself in your head. Everything going on around us exists both in reality and in our mind. Our perception of reality is just a story our mind tells us about a person, event or situation. Sometimes that story is accurate. Other times, it's completely off base, but how we respond is a product of that self-talk.

If you see a pretty girl, you might tell yourself, "Wow, I'd like to get to know her. She's just my type." Or you might say, "I could never talk to someone like her. She's too hot for me." How you think about the girl will dictate what you do. All she does is stand there and look good.

Anger often comes from other emotions, and if you can't identify those, you won't be able to reconcile them or your anger.

The same is true of an anger-producing situation. If your teacher gives you a bad grade, you may think "What a witch. She's doing this because she hates me. I'm through trying in her class." This is called "attribution" and it is the root of most angry responses. Tell yourself something more rational like, "Wow, that witch is making this difficult. I'm going to have to study harder next time to show her she can't get to me." The angry feeling is still there, but now it generates energy toward a more productive response.

If you listen to your internal dialog, you'll find some thoughts agitate you and others pacify you. Replace the agitating thoughts with calming, pacifying ones that reduce your anger. Here's a couple of examples for you to practice:

"My mom is late. She ruined my whole day" versus "That's my mom. Late again. What's it matter in the larger scheme of things?"

"I can't stand how that guy always talks down to me," versus "How pathetic for him that he treats others this way." In the latter case, the problem belongs to him. In the former, you're taking everything personally.

"My parents totally favor my brother over me" versus "My brother got the good deal this time, but I remember when I had their favor."

Psychologists also warn against making too many "should statements" that place unrealistic demands on you and everyone else. We just don't live in a world where we can control other people and events just because they should do what we want or what is right. And no matter how mad we get, nothing is going to change that. Teach yourself to avoid "shoulds" and focus instead on statements like, "It's dumb to think others will always act the way I want them to" or "I can't control how they act by getting pissed, so why get all worked up?"

I know this looks great on paper, and is harder to do in real life. However, with some practice, you can actually talk yourself out of anger-producing, self-defeating thoughts, and the actions that go with them.

You'll find yourself a great deal more powerful as a result.

John Murray: I think of collecting anger like collecting stamps. Whenever someone upsets you, you can choose to print out "anger stamps" which you later redeem for a furious rampage. Or you can opt not to print the stamps in the first place.

Make sure you understand what is really upsetting you. Anger often comes from other emotions, and if you can't identify those emotions, you won't be able to reconcile them or your anger. Depression in men is underreported because they mask it with anger. In talking with your therapist, put all your issues on the table so as to present an accurate picture of your entire psyche.

Anger is also related to anxiety, sometimes referred to as "frozen fear," because it's much easier to get angry when you're scared. Students may be testy during exam season and couples tend to get in fights when big issues like money come into play. Sometimes the fear of not being wanted can trigger anger. For example, if you forget your brother's birthday, he'll probably be a lot more understanding than your girlfriend would be if you forgot her special day. That's because your relationship with your brother is stable and he won't worry about your long term prospects. Your girlfriend, however, might think you don't care about her anymore and even fear a looming breakup.

If fear causes anger, then we need to fight fear to fight anger. Talk to your therapist about what makes you afraid, whether it's money, school, parents, or anything else. As Wes said, a change in perspective can help sooth your anger and increase your emotional competence.

Problem Eating

Dear Dr. Wes and John,

In your opinion, does the media play a role in the incidence of anorexia or bulimia among teenage girls? How about being overweight? Do you think girls get the idea that they must look like the stick-thin models so they will "fit in" or be able to get a hot boyfriend? Does the media portray overweight women to be "bad" people in society?

Dr. Wes: Eating disorders are much more complex than that. I've read research and attended training on this topic and there's simply no one thing that causes anorexia, bulimia, or overeating. Clearly, the media plays a role by portraying the golden mean of feminine beauty as the thin sixteen-year-old girl. If you don't believe me, take a look at most magazine covers in any given month. Our society sells "sexy" as the *image* of teenage girls, regardless of the real age of the model, and then complain when girls and young women try to live up to that. Moreover, teenagers buy media that is more appropriate for older, more mature, and more sophisticated consumers. So, very young teens and even "tweenies" read *Seventeen*, while the mid-teens have already moved on to *Cosmo*. The same is true for television. Kids "watch up" to learn what the next developmental phase holds for them, and it turns out that much of TV's message is "be thin and pretty, thin and pretty, thin and pretty"—like a really harmful mantra.

Kids see this illusion of a perfect body and say "hey, I can do that."

However, to prove that the media is at the root of eating problems you'd have to see more kids with eating disorders than we have, and they'd have to be free of other problems. Instead, there are usually specific family dynamics associated with eating disorders, which often involve high achievement orientation and low conflict resolution. They raise kids who appear on the surface to be "really good" kids. Instead of acting out, they turn inward and try to control other aspects of their lives. That's where the media comes in. Kids see this illusion of a perfect body and say "hey, I can do that." This is a ultra-short explanation for a very complicated issue, but it gives you a flavor of how eating disorders work. Getting rid of fashion mags isn't going to solve the issue.

The media may also create unintended problems in a more subtle way, with very good intentions. There's a growing focus on obesity as a serious threat to the health of millions of adults, children and teens. This has the dual effect of waking up some folks and saving their lives, and making others feel even worse about themselves, which in turn makes them *less* likely to find a healthier lifestyle.

Bottom line: A healthy weight is easy to calculate, sometimes difficult to achieve, and rarely well-covered in the media. It depends on many factors and how you perceive and invest in them.

John Murray: There's no doubt our commercial media conveys a warped female image. Women on magazine covers are drawn from a few dozen models handpicked from a sample of three billion women. Each has been completely made-over twice, first by professional makeup and hair stylists, then with digital-imaging technology. The media has started to report the backlash, but that hasn't stopped them from broadcasting the same old thing. The Associated Press recently ran an article claiming sexed up images hurt young women's self-esteem, along with a photograph of four swimsuit models' backsides.

Whatever its cause, doctors agree the condition is serious. The teen years are a period of physical growth, so cutting off the body's nutritional supply line can permanently impact maturation. Low blood sugar levels reduce your ability to think clearly and prevent you from developing new lines of thought, making other life problems even more difficult. Even more serious, anorexia has been linked to osteoporosis, bruising, and immune deficiency. The effects of starvation on the body add up and one in ten anorexics eventually die from the disorder.

If you find yourself struggling with eating issues, *please* tell a responsible adult. Psychologists know how to work with this problem, and they can help you if you seek help first. Girls need to reassure friends with self-image problems and lend an ear to those who feel overwhelmed or ostracized. Guys need to be more sensitive and stop comparing their girlfriends to an impossible ideal, or even worse, pornography.

Everyday Suicide Prevention

Dr. Wes: While suicide is the third leading cause of death among teens (ranking behind accidents and murder), it remains thankfully rare. About 1,500 teens are known to commit suicide in a given year in the United States. Each incident asks us to reexamine our communities and ourselves to consider why it happens at all.

Though we've shared them before[9], I worry that lists of warning signs actually limit our ability to help those in distress. Lists ironically yield both false-positives and false security at the same time, offering no substitute for the real and crucial connections we need to make with one another. Lists are easy. Understanding is not. Lists also make the families and friends of suicide victims feel guilty, believing they "should have seen the signs," when that's rarely true.

We're supposed to ask ourselves three questions before we say something: Is it kind? Is it true? Is it necessary?

I have a better idea. One we can each practice every day without a list. Let's consider anyone as having a potential for self-harm, given the right set of circumstances and stressors, with teens being especially vulnerable to loneliness, alienation, and self-destructive thinking. Only then can we see that the best response is to value each other every day; reach out kindly; consider how we impact the lives around us; take seriously our individual power to harm and help.

In his young adult novel, *Thirteen Reasons Why*, Jay Asher addresses this issue quite poignantly. It reminds us that we are all interconnected and, to an extent, responsible for each other in our words and actions. Yet increasingly, teenagers follow adults in our society, showing a

---

[9] That column is found in Chapter 5 of *Dear Dr. Wes...Real Life Advice for Parents of Teens* under the title "Suicidal Thoughts."

callous disregard for personal dignity and human suffering in favor of a perverted version of free speech that often comes anonymously and without personal responsibility. Texting, email, and Facebook make harsh interactions impersonal, as if writing it down and sending it makes it okay.

Only a tiny fraction of teens will respond to difficulties by taking their own lives, but many will consider it. Each of us has a responsibility to help each other find a better way, lead one another toward a sense of self-worth, and emphasize the worth of others. No one is responsible for suicide except the person committing it, and I'm not suggesting otherwise. But the choices we make in our daily interactions belong to each of us. Make them humanely.

Samantha Schwartz: In high school, almost everyone knows someone who has thought about committing suicide. Some have issues at home or within themselves that none of us can control. For others, the problem lies with interpersonal relationships. We've all heard about cases of teens killing themselves because they've been bullied by classmates.

I would venture to say that 90% of people are not mean-spirited or intentionally hurtful. So how do the cruel 10% get away with what they do? It's the followers. They stand by and allow it to happen without blinking an eye. I hate to be a cynic, but I've come to believe that followers make up most of the population, and yet it's hard to blame them. Taking a stand is scary; no one wants to risk being the next target.

I'm no Gandhi. I've slipped into bashing someone so excruciatingly annoying that I convinced myself he's brought it upon himself. We need to realize that just like academic intelligence, there is social intelligence, and some people just aren't very gifted. They have trouble picking up social cues, so they behave in ways we find odd or irritating. I'm still developing patience for these people. Sometimes what I say feels like word vomit—awful things flowing out of my mouth without my control. But I do have control. It's a matter of training myself to think before I speak.

My mom once had a notepad with yoga's *Principles of Mindful Speech* written on them. I think they're dead on. We're supposed to ask ourselves three questions before we say something: Is it kind? Is it true? Is it necessary? When tempted to pile on complaints about someone, thinking through these questions can help slow down the thought process and let the right words come to the surface.

It's definitely a challenge, and I don't always succeed. However, when I feel guilty for talking badly about someone, I try to reverse it by looking for something I like about her and complimenting her on it. I see it as tipping the scale of someone's day slightly toward the positive. We all weigh our days subconsciously, counting up the good and bad things to give it a final rating.

Those days add up.

People who consider suicide feel their lives are tipped toward the negative. We each have the ability to add some weight on the positive side.

Secret of Happiness

Julia Davidson: Recently, while at the library, I decided to stray from my normal novel-seeking routine and hunt down something new. I found the psychology section and began to look at some of the titles. Most turned out to be books about self-help and wellbeing. I found, I kid you not, books on how to become happy in eight days, seven steps, or three minutes (as well as various other measures of time).

That got me thinking. Can following the rules someone else lays down for you really produce happiness? And if it works, is it because of the procedures you followed or because someone with a PhD said they would work? And what portion of this advice is based on proven endorphin-releasing techniques like eating dark chocolate, exercising, or laughing? How much takes a little trickery on the part of the person writing the book and the person reading it? Sure, you can down all the Hershey bars, exercise tapes, and comedy tracks you want, but I doubt happiness can be produced with a simple set of techniques.

If you think about it, doctors and mental health providers are trusted figures in society. People are apt to believe, try, or take something, if the doc says it's good. Those who write these books present themselves as happy, successful people in the world. Otherwise, we wouldn't be reading their advice. If a death row criminal wrote a self-help book, I doubt anyone would take it seriously. Certainly, their thoughts may be as worthy as anyone else's, but people aren't going to put much faith in their judgment on this subject. So, there's trick number one: People believe that by taking the advice of a well-rounded, happy person, they too will become well-rounded and happy.

Monkey see, monkey do.

People also want happiness fast, hence a certain number of steps, minutes, or easy techniques guaranteeing euphoria in the near future. It's like believing that taking one pill for an illness will make you feel a little better, so taking more will make you feel a lot better. Such is the case with self-help. If drinking cranberry juice and walking your dog once a day produces happiness in a week, why not do both three times a day? Besides causing indigestion, this makes people think they are getting results faster. Trick number two: Self-help books cater to immediate results by making their techniques as short and sweet as possible.

Believe in yourself, but also listen to others. Take intelligent risks. Stay curious about your limits and how to challenge them. Search for meaning.

Happiness is subjective. Self-help books are really kind of ironic if you think about it: someone else's self-produced happiness solution, written for you.

Dr. Wes: In my line of work, as a well-rounded and successful PhD who dispenses self-produced happiness advice, this issue pops up about twice a day. While Julia is right—happiness is subjective—the folks coming into my office don't greet that answer with much enthusiasm. They get frustrated if the therapist hasn't thought these things through. I'm sure that fuels the market for self-help books.

So, what's Dr. Wes's fabulous principle of happiness, the one that applies across diverse people and cultures, and can be delivered right to your door. Drum roll please...

Organization.

I feel a strange sense of yawning. I guess my shot at the self-help book market isn't "Three-Day" or "7-Habit" enough.

Seriously, though, if you look across a large sample of people, you'll find that the happiest folks aren't the richest, best looking, or smartest. They're the ones who've organized their lives in such a way as to create a meaningful and rewarding existence. It's that simple.

I don't mean they know where their car keys are or have a smartphone with all their appointments on it, though both of those things make *me* really happy. I mean they've made decisions and plans, have goals, hopes, dreams, and a realistic way of approaching the world, so that even the struggle toward fulfillment is meaningful.

Organization can involve many things, but it nearly always includes decisions about career and education, who we choose to love, and how we develop our social network. It often involves how we manage family relationships, especially in adolescence and early adulthood. Of course, biology creates some openings or obstacles for feeling good, making choices, and following through on our plans, but in the end, free will accounts for a big portion of our happiness. More importantly, none of us can control our genetics or the social class into which we're born. We can only control our everyday choices, and how we organize our life by making them.

Rather than purchasing a book that teaches you how to trick yourself into being happy, give this whole organization theory a try. How it looks will vary from person to person, but what it can do is very powerful. Believe in yourself, but also listen to others. Take intelligent risks. Keep at it until you succeed. Stay curious about your limits and how to challenge them. Search for meaning.

Is mine the true path to happiness or just more tricky thinking?

I say it doesn't matter as long as the product turns out fine.

6 SCHOOL

Hate for Teacher

Dear Dr. Wes and Marissa,

I don't like my teacher, so I don't work hard in her class. What should I do?

Marissa Ballard: It's not uncommon for kids to dislike their teachers. Many teachers don't even seem to like kids. So, it's puzzling that they chose a profession where they're with children every single day. Though your teacher may not brighten your life, her attitude is no excuse for you to do poorly in her class.

Not liking your teacher has nothing to do with your academic performance. Consider it an opportunity to be the best student in the class. There's a sense of triumph in acing a test given by a particularly snooty teacher, and I'm sure you'll enjoy it immensely, if you give yourself the chance.

This class should be viewed as an individual challenge not only academically, but to your character as well. You'll always have to deal with people whom you don't like. Someday, it might even be your boss. While working for this teacher might not always be delightful, if you learn to have patience and not take her attitude personally, you might be better equipped to handle this and future situations.

If you allow people you do not like or with whom you disagree to negatively influence you, it will be hard to succeed at anything. You won't have this teacher forever, but the grade you receive will remain long after your last test. After freshmen year, every semester grade you receive counts toward your accumulative high school GPA, and a few bad marks can hold you back.

You're not being forced to get an education by a dictatorial school system. You're being offered free schooling for the last time in your life.

I look back at my ninth grade Geometry class and cringe. It's the only class in which I ever received a C-minus, and I wish I could go back and change it. So, stick with it. In the end, you'll feel better about yourself than had you allowed yourself to fail.

Dr. Wes: You have things backwards here. You're not being forced to get an education by a dictatorial school system. You're being offered free schooling for the last time in your life. So, it's your job to dig until you find the cool gift of learning buried underneath all the crap.

I was not always so clever about this myself. In fact, I hated school at your age. I left the big city in sixth grade and spent the rest of my school years in a small school where everyone knew everyone from the day they were born. It was not an easy place to get a good education when your science teacher spent most of the period discussing last night's basketball game. My rebel friend and I referred to our school as the "indoctrination center," intended to churn out mental clones of the people in charge. I seem to recall listening to a lot of Pink Floyd's *The Wall*, too.

Anyway, I realized something during all this. You can't let other people's shortcomings make you mediocre. You're not a puppet. You are in charge of your education. Find the good teachers in your school and build your schedule around their classes. Learn to turn bad classes into a test of wills, kind of like academic chicken. The teacher tries to deny you an education and you use all your teen rebellion to force him to give you the best possible one. Make them explain things to you. Write better papers than they ask you to write so you can educate them on all the things they don't seem to understand. Ask the best questions just to make them look up the answers and rethink their teaching.

I've done this myself over the years. Sometimes it gained me respect, and sometimes it just got me in trouble. But in the end, I was the winner because I not only graduated but also learned something about myself. Marissa is correct—if you do this right, you'll get a great ego boost by proving your capacity to learn even when no one is teaching. Just be careful not to appear arrogant, because that ultimately loses the battle for you.

School is pretty much like the rest of life. Some folks you want to hang out with and be like, and some you don't. Your job is to find as many of those in the first category and let them influence you. Aside from my parents, the most influential people in my life have been teachers. Some—my fifth grade teacher, two high school English teachers and several of my college and grad school professors—inspired me to become who I am today, an author and a psychologist.

Others influenced me with their ignorance, poor character, and lack of love for learning or teaching. Yet, I'm glad I knew them, too. They taught me what not to be.

Your education is sacred. Don't let anyone take it from you.

Intellectual Self-Esteem

Samantha Schwartz:

Dear Smart Women,

Remember in elementary school how we spoke up in class and asked questions without stopping to filter ourselves? In middle school, a strange thing happened. We stopped raising our hands and started becoming more self-conscious about our intelligence. We forgot what it felt like to beam with pride when we guessed right.

My New Year's Resolution is to do three calculus problems on the board and call out two guesses in AP Physics.

What changed us? Let's start with an ugly truth about our supposedly gender-neutral society. A smart girl is not treated the same as a smart guy. At worst, he might be labeled "cocky," while a girl may be labeled controlling and aggressive. Some of us are silent because we want to be liked.

Other girls want to be the best just as much as the boys do, yet remain silent because they are self-conscious. In math and science especially, we choose not to speak in class out of a fear of being wrong, even if we get A's and understand the material. We choose to treat each question as a referendum on our intelligence, worrying that others are judging us. Our inner perfectionist stops us from saying something we're thinking because we don't want to look stupid.

I'm not sure why we girls seem to experience this anxiety more strongly than our male peers. When my guy friends think they might have an answer, they go ahead and blurt it out, even if they aren't called on. And they don't seem to care if they get it wrong. We whisper our guesses to each other, lacking the guts to share them with the class.

Still others among us choose to be silent out of respect for other students, giving them time to think through the answer without interruption. But this courtesy is not always necessary and, in some instances, functions as a way for us to hide our smarts or avoid taking a risk. We need to remember that, sometimes, one of us girls really is the only one who knows the answer and that being wrong on occasion is as much a part of learning as being right.

Can we solve this problem? Can we change society and girls' intellectual identities? I can only tell you what I will do. My New Year's Resolution is to do three calculus problems on the board and call out two guesses in AP Physics.

What's yours?

Sincerely, Samantha

Dr. Wes:

Dear Samantha,

Good luck with your important goal. I'll bug you about it along the way, encouraging you to be as excited about your mistakes and the learning they hold, as your successes. It's easy to recite old saws—nothing ventured, nothing gained; anyone who's never made a mistake has never tried anything new, and so on. It's harder to live them out in the unforgiving world of middle and high school.

As you point out, the core of the problem is a reluctance to take healthy risks. That's not only a gender issue, but an educational one. We've put all our eggs in the basket of grades and standardized testing, and I have terrible news for you: That's not education, it's just evaluation. We learn almost nothing by taking tests or getting good grades. We learn by trying, succeeding and failing, and trying something different;

by solving problems with unique ideas; and by researching what others have done and stretching their conclusions.

Our schools would do well to reward students for superior *effort* rather than for the percentage of questions they answered correctly. But that's not what schools are allowed to do. They're on the same hamster wheel you are. They get graded too, but never for their efforts. And, if anything, this focus on achievement (rather than effort) only worsens the gender differences you cite.

Since that's not going to change, it's good that you want to influence your peers, particularly those young women who may be less assertive in advocating for their own education. In a true academic environment, students are supportive colleagues who challenge each other to think out of the box, venture a guess, and try again when they crash. And don't forget that this goes beyond the advanced placement college-bound girls. Everyone benefits from a safe environment where we can stretch ourselves and meet the academic demands of any given subject—be it music, art, writing, auto mechanics, welding, or whatever.

Finally, Samantha, I wish all students saw themselves as consumers of the valuable commodity of education—just as you do. My cousin graduated from Central High School in Little Rock, Arkansas when I was in eighth grade. Just fifteen years earlier the National Guard escorted nine frightened black kids up Central's front steps in one of the early skirmishes inspired by the Civil Rights Movement. After my cousin's graduation, Dad led me down those same steps and told me the story, adding, "That's how much those kids wanted a good education."

Maybe today's girls aren't standing up for their right to learn—taking risks, asking questions, and demanding they be heard—because they've never known what it's like to have those rights threatened or denied. They don't realize the consequences of staying on the sidelines. I'm not saying we should return to those scary times just to make a point. Just remember them and take advantage of the amazing chance we now have for a free quality education.

And so, Samantha, I close my letter with a final challenge. Remember, and help your friends remember, that school may be a royal pain, but education never is. Find every opportunity to overcome the learning obstacles we've created for you, as well as the ones you've imagined for yourselves. What strength you'll find inside yourself when you face the fear of failure and embrace it as a tool of learning!

Best Wishes for Your Intellectual Success, Wes

Teachers Didn't Notice

Dear Dr. Wes and John,

Last year I struggled to complete and turn in my assignments. Beginning this semester, I started a new medication for ADHD, which helps me a lot. Recently, we were informed there will be a pizza party for all students who complete and turned in all of their assignments. Today, the money for the pizza was due, but when I tried to turn mine in, my teacher told me I had not completed one of my science labs. Puzzled, I left. I could have sworn I turned this in. Missing out on the party was not what bothered me. It was the fact that my teachers didn't notice my progress. Before, they had to hound me about missing work, but now that I've improved, they haven't said anything. How can I tell them this without seeming snooty?

Dr. Wes: Nothing is more frustrating than struggling against a difficult obstacle, succeeding and then having everyone ignore your achievement, especially those who were pressing for the change. It can make your efforts seem futile. I've seen this with parents, teachers, boy- and girlfriends, husbands and wives. People believe that if they expect a reasonable change, then they needn't get too excited if someone makes it. But this isn't the way things work. Kid's, especially those with ADHD or other learning problems, need consistent encouragement and reward to stay motivated. Simply put, you probably need the pizza *more* than the kids who find school easy to manage.

Unfortunately, you're facing a larger problem inherent in our educational system. Teachers today are quite overburdened. Our local, state and federal governments are all on their backs, demanding that they do more, faster, with fewer resources, lower pay, and more students per class. If students ever get a pizza party, it's a rare day indeed. This leads many teachers to essentially run from one fire to the next, trying to keep class functioning. They saw your fire (poor school performance), and now they are happy that you put it out. "OK, time to move on to the next big thing…"

While this doesn't excuse their failure to give you praise, it may explain it. If I were you, I'd drop in after school and tell your teachers in a kind way exactly what you wrote above, that pizza or no pizza you'd like to be recognized for your efforts. And be sure to tell them that you value their opinions of you. That alone might make their day.

I've suggested to many parents that they reward their kid's effort (time studying) rather than the result (grades). This usually generates more effort, which ultimately produces better results. Unfortunately, as you've found out, it's hard to get schools to have that kind of conversion for one simple reason: Effort is a lot harder to measure than outcome, and the U.S. Department of Education is basically after better scores on those standardized tests.

That said, I'd be the first to drop off a pizza gift card at your doorstep. Keep up the good work.

John Murray: As Lawrence Kohlberg said, recognition is one of the prime wants for humans. What you are looking for is trust and respect from your family and community, who've long considered you an underachiever. However, recognition takes a long time to build and they may suspect you'll fall back into your old ways. It's not your fault that you had a medical disorder which prevented you from staying organized, but such circumstances are sometimes lost in the shuffle and may even become yet another reason to unfairly judge others.

Here are some ways you can draw attention to your hard work. Try to do well on group assignments and oral reports, which are often the most attention-garnering projects. Regularly ask your teachers what assignments you're missing, providing them an opportunity to comment on your improving performance. You may also need a clearer goal. If your parents and teachers set a vague standard for you, such as "completing and submitting work in an adequate and timely manner," try making the goal more specific, like getting a certain GPA. That way, it will be clear when you cross the threshold.

I admire you for making the effort to solve not one, but two, problems. However, since you forgot to turn in a science project, you're not out of the woods yet. Experiment with organizational systems. Write everything down, use a different folder for each of your classes, and fill out your assignment books. Install time-management software on your computer, or better yet, get a smartphone and program it to send you reminders about upcoming due dates. My father swears by it.

Even though we pretend not to care what parents and adults think, we really do seek their approval. Providing a positive incentive is a great way to keep us happy and focused on success.

School Bored

Dear Dr. Wes and Julia,

I am having a difficult time staying invested in my classes this year. The subject matter is easier than I expected, so I now find myself fighting the urge to skip. Whenever I do attend, it's almost painful to sit through because I am so bored and feel like I'm wasting my time. Any suggestions on how to keep myself focused and interested?

Julia Davidson: From the first day of kindergarten, you can tell what kind of student you're going to be: a school lover, one who just tolerates school, or a school hater. My first day was one of the happiest of my life, but lately I've needed a cup of coffee, two breaks during the school day, and the promise of a fun rehearsal *after* school to rouse me in the morning. School gets less and less fun as the years go by and more is expected of you, including the expectation that you even want to learn the material. I struggled through many classes, so here are a few tricks that kept me somewhat focused, or at least learning, throughout the years.

TV, iPods, text messaging, Facebook, cell phones, school and community activities. Compared to these activities, school is mind-numbingly boring.

Try to study with friends. Not only did my study group give me a better understanding of the material, but I got a rap song about photosynthesis out of it. You might also ask the teacher to have a student lead classes once in a while. By teaching or having a fellow student teach, you learn the material your way. You can take new educational liberties by using Power Points, creating skits or utilizing other alternative learning strategies.

Another trick is to have something to take your mind off school as often as you can, and still maintain academically. Involve yourself in an activity that you can look forward to during the day, maybe a study hall where you can relax a little or zone out for a second every now and then. Having a "perfectly-focused-student" mindset all day ends up being self-destructive, so let yourself take small mental breaks over the course of the day. Think of it as a catnap for the brain.

Tips like these—plus the ones you invent for yourself—can help you retain and stay interested in the material you're learning, or at least keep going to school after that first day of kindergarten.

Dr. Wes: It's hard to say for sure what's bugging you. It could be a lot of things. However, one thing I commonly see these days is more a sociological factor than a psychological one. I don't have a clever name for it, but it comes from growing up in the most overstimulated generation in history. TV, iPods, text messaging, Facebook, cell phones, countless school and community activities, and high levels of socializing all conspire to train the mind to seek out novelty and spectacle. Compared to these activities, school is mind-numbingly boring.

Many educators try hard to compete, though. These same technologies in the hands of a skilled teacher can make learning a lot easier and more fun. Still, for most kids, school is more like a job than recreation. Do you know anyone who pops up like toast every morning and skips to their job while singing a happy tune? That's what I thought.

I was a pretty good student, but from seventh grade to senior year of high school, I can guarantee you that when April 1st hit, I was literally counting the days 'til the end of school...23, 22, 21. And when that last day came, I hit the door like a bat out of hell. Three months later—we actually had *three months* of summer back in the day—I dreaded going back because I felt like I was "so bored and wasting my time."

What kept me going was not what I had on my academic plate that day. It was the idea that there must be something worthwhile down the road, a better tomorrow out there in adultland, and that high school and college were necessary parts of reaching it. So, school became a journey, and somehow I ended up there ten years longer than I'd planned, despite my lack of enthusiasm.

Except for a few wonderful experiences that you'll always cherish, school will tend to vacillate between stressful and boring. Try not to waste time running down too many blind alleys. They'll just add to your frustration. Take at least one class every semester that gives you energy rather than sucking it out of you. Maybe it's computers, music, media, or woodshop. If you love history or math, you might find your energy there, which will make it a little easier to suffer through English. I realize it's getting harder to take electives nowadays, but hopefully you can find one class worthy of popping up in the morning.

Despite popular lore, how we feel about life isn't as important as what we choose to do with it. Looking back, I'm deeply thankful that my family encouraged my education, and despite more than a few potholes in the road, it's been a worthwhile trip.

Sharing Grades

Samantha Schwartz: Teachers use a wide variety of threats to quiet students, but nothing is as effective as the tense silence they create just before handing back tests. Then, the moment the first test lands on a desk, the silence evaporates and the whispering starts.

I can usually guess how others did by their facial expressions. A quick glance, then the corners of the mouth turning upward—good news. Furrowed eyebrows, eyes scanning the same thing over and over—bad news.

Should you take it further and ask your peers how they did? To some this is akin to a full body scan at the airport. For others, asking questions about grades is a habit. My rule is don't ask, but here are my exceptions:

- **Everyone did terribly.** If everyone is talking about how hard a test was and you agree, share your thoughts. Weirdly enough, hard tests often become good class bonding moments.
- **You're still confused.** If you still don't get some of the test questions, finding someone who got an "A" will help you figure things out. If you paid any attention in class, you can probably predict who would be comfortable sharing her good grade.
- **You studied with someone else.** If you prepared for the test with a friend, it's fine to want to know how he did. It may help you realize whether studying together worked.
- **Another person shared without prompting.** At this point, it's your choice whether to disclose your score. It's perfectly appropriate not to, which will let the other person know that you're not open to that discussion. But this does give you the green light if you want to share.

Otherwise, comparing yourself to others is unhealthy. If you did your best and the test shows it, you don't need to know everyone else's scores to validate the greatness of your own. If your test results are undesirable, it's better to discuss the score with your teacher than to brood over it with others. A score is just a number, but how you behave in this kind of situation is a reflection of your character.

Dr. Wes: Toward the end of graduate school a professor who was really big on writing warned the class he would never give anything higher than a "C" on first drafts of our major research paper. The day he handed back those drafts, he paused at my desk and announced to the other sixty people in attendance that my paper was the rare exception. I liked the big fat "A" and his kind words and he certainly meant no harm. But I could almost hear my colleagues, those folks you depend on like family in grad school, groaning and gnashing their teeth. And it wasn't a pleasant sound.

Moral of the story: When grades are shared, you lose if you win and you lose if you lose. Good or bad, they're only your business.

Once you've graduated and are out in the workforce, trade school, or college, nobody is ever going to care what your grades were in high school. After you land your first job, the same is true for college. No one comes to my office and asks me why I got a "C" in Biological Psychology. They just care about whether I know the material.

Unfortunately, we've begun to treat grades as if they mean something more than their original intent: feedback on how you're doing in a class; a suggestion on how to do better. That's it. Nothing to show off or hide from. Yes, I realize college-bound students need a good GPA, but there's more to college application than that, and the research on going to "the right school" shows it isn't all it's cracked up to be.

That said, there is actually one very good reason to keep track of everyone else's performance. Without dipping too far into statistics, it's called norm referencing, meaning you compare your score to the group as a whole. Beyond the bonding moment Sam mentions, knowing how you compare to others is usually more important than just knowing your raw score. That's how the ACT and SAT are constructed. It's also important in evaluating instruction and assessment in a class. Students are *consumers* of education and have a right to expect a normal distribution of scores across the semester to be sure the teaching and material are a good fit for the grade level. If say, 90% of the students get a "C" or below on a test, something is wrong with either the instruction or the test. Conversely, too many "As," and the class is too easy.

If instead you're one of a handful getting "Ds," then you need to step up the effort or ask whether you're in the right class. The only way to know this is to understand where you fit into the curve. And unless grades are anonymously posted, which really is pretty helpful, that requires some discussion with classmates.

All this good advice may end up being purely academic, no pun intended. People are naturally curious about their performance in anything they do, well beyond any rational need to know. So, I bet you'll keep right on sharing.

Very Advanced Placement

Dear Dr. Wes and Ben,

I'm twelve but already in high school through accelerated placement. I was recently accepted to a prestigious high school summer camp, but because of my age the director won't let me room with the other students. The director wrote me and said, "Can you think of any sixteen-year-old who would want to room with someone who has not even entered puberty, no matter how smart she is? A sixteen-year-old would want to be with her own peers." Do you think society should support early achievers such as myself in associating with people at older ages?

Dr. Wes: As a psychologist, I have very mixed feelings about your situation. It's been my clinical experience that, on average, advanced grade placement is not in the best interests of young people and I always advise against it. There are numerous education enhancement programs available in our area and I tend to favor them. This is because both intellectual capacity and emotional maturity must align with development, and while the former can be hurried, the latter cannot. Development occurs within a social context, not solely within the individual. So, I imagine you're just seeing the tip of the iceberg regarding how others will receive you as you matriculate through high school and into college.

Don't let anyone's ignorance hold you back.

That said, I believe the director of this camp was both insensitive and wrong. The program you described in your extended letter is performance-based and you got in. As a former camp counselor myself, I most certainly *can* imagine a properly selected sixteen-year-old who would enjoy having a "kid sister" as a roommate, especially one with your gifts and talents. As long as you are sensitive to the developmental differences I mentioned and accept that you are not yet a full-fledged teenager, the director should encourage you and help match you with a teen leader who's not afraid to try something a little different this summer.

You have many adventures ahead. Despite my reservations, I am impressed with your initiative. Don't let anyone's ignorance hold you back.

Ben Markley: Maturity varies from person to person, and not just as a function of age. An ethics professor may still be a selfish bully; a high school dropout may offer better counsel than a scholar. Intellect and emotions certainly influence each other, yet we make a mistake when we assume that their growth is parallel. Wes is correct, a hypothetical ten-year-old with college-level math skills is still, in many important ways, a ten-year-old.

A friend of mine recently told me about a friend of hers who had incredible reading and verbal skills when he was very young and, consequently, was expected to behave socially at the same accelerated level. This led to emotional and intellectual confusion that still haunts him to this day. This is the danger of assuming a fully rounded maturity in a young person of great intelligence.

I'm not saying that everyone is confined to the average maturity of their age group, and everyone benefits from associating with people of different ages, particularly in a mentorship. While these kinds of situations should be considered on a case-by-case basis, I see no solid basis for placing all early achievers into older academic or friendship groups.

7 FRIENDSHIP

Real Friends

Dr. Wes: You won't be surprised to learn that a big part of my job working with teenagers is helping them navigate the complex map of social life in middle and high school. Since adolescence includes a big helping of sexual energy, kids devote a lot of time to honing their skills as romantic couples. But an even larger chunk goes into figuring out how to bond with friends, which turns out to be an even more difficult task. The teen "dating" world actually follows some fairly predictable rules. Friendship does not.

It's harder to guide kids toward making and keeping close friendships in part because your social groups look a lot like European alliances just before World War I. You jockey for position in the social hierarchy, and any false move can set things off in the wrong direction. This gets a little *Worry less about how popular someone makes you look or feel.* better toward the end of high school, but social drama often extends well into college.

In response to this, my best advice goes against every fiber of your social culture. Pay attention to the authentic people you have a chance to hang out with, and worry less about how popular someone makes you look or feel. Too often, real friends aren't the people who know how to claw their way to the top and stay there. They're the ones who keep your secrets, don't undercut you in the dating pool, and give back as much as they take in the relationship. They notice your authentic self and show more interest in that than the mask you wear to get through the day.

Those are the friendships that endure, and the ones you'll take with you for the rest of your life.

Miranda Davis: Wes is right. Real friends—the ones who will have your back, stick up for you, and always stand by your side—can be hard to find. These are the people with whom you will actually want to stay in touch once you leave high school.

There's no problem with having people at work, in class, and on sports teams whom you just get along with, but beware of situational or fair-weather friends. Don't get too attached to a relationship that's just convenient for you or the other person. If there isn't any actual bonding, don't expect the relationship to last long. Those situations offer great opportunities to meet people, but for a real friendship to develop you have to put yourself out there and take a risk. It's a lot harder to make friends if you're not friendly.

It might sound corny, but making real friends also means being yourself. The only way to connect with someone who likes your personality is to reveal that personality. If you take classes and get involved in clubs and extracurricular activities that you enjoy, you're bound to meet people who are similar to you. True friends know that friendship is a two-way street. If you aren't a real friend to someone, they won't be one to you.

Ditched

Dear Dr. Wes and Marissa,

I'm a senior girl and I have two friends whom I consider to be my best friends, or so I thought. Over the last few months, they have started ditching me almost completely, and instead they hang out with each other and their boyfriends, which totally annoys me. I have confronted both of them about this two different times, and yet nothing has changed at all. So, now I don't know what to do. A large part of me wants to say screw them and be completely done with it, but a small part is afraid to end the friendships, even though I kind of think I should. So, what should I do?

Dr. Wes: In forming my response, I'm assuming there aren't other factors affecting this situation. For example, your friends being legitimately upset with you and using their boyfriends as a pretense to ditch you. If after a careful self-analysis you're pretty sure things are otherwise cool, then you have to judge them by their words and actions. Apparently, they're caught up in wild romances now and hanging out with a b.f.f. can't compare. Try not to take this too personally. It's pretty common and probably not about you.

I happen to think your friends' approach isn't a great idea for young women of your age group. In fact, boyfriends seem to be the number one reason girlfriends split up. While I applaud exclusivity in a world of rampant hooking-up, I worry girls are losing out on important relationships with peers.

Friendships deteriorate quickly with lack of interest, particularly among teen girls. In other cases, girls fight it out (literally and figuratively) over guys, ruining friendships that have lasted since grade school. Lately, the old adage that no guy is worth coming between two friends has gone out the window as girls seem increasingly less interested in maintaining healthy friendships. Research shows that this is a big mistake.

You have to nurture any relationship to keep it going. If your friends don't put forth that effort, maybe it's time to get some new ones. Just don't get mad and tell them off on the way out. They may grow out of this and someday you'll want to hang out with them again. Just start looking to see who else is interesting and strike up new friendships with them.

Eventually, your friends will realize how much they've isolated themselves and will end up regretting it.

Alternatively, you might want to hang out less often with the old friends over the next year, then graduate and find a new crowd at college or work. Some of this tapers off by then, as young adults strive for a more balanced life. After high school, you'll find a lot more people with whom to share your life.

Marissa Ballard: I've had this situation happen with numerous friends and there's not much you can do about it. It's understandable that you are hurt by their lack of interest, but try to not take it to heart. Every teen girl I've known has gotten wrapped up in her relationships to the point that friends take a back seat.

You have a couple of options. You could stay angry and decide to end the friendships yourself. While you might think it would be hard to find two new best friends, I'm sure there are plenty of other girls you could spend time with and become closer to. A better option might be to just relax and let them come around in their own time. Pursue other interests and activities and you might end up meeting new friends in the process. Not hanging out as often shouldn't automatically mean that you're no longer friends.

Like Wes said, most middle and high school relationships come to an end. Eventually, your friends will realize how much they've isolated themselves and will end up regretting it. Don't feel bad about the fact they drifted from you. Use this experience to help you remain aware of your own actions toward others and to avoid the same problems when you start dating someone.

Shyness

John Murray: If I could have a super power, it would be the ability to detect and avoid my own awkwardness from miles away. There are many reasons people are shy, but the most prominent one is a fear of looking awkward in front of peers, or saying something stupid and losing face. Meeting people requires an investment of time and confidence, and some teens don't want to risk rejection.

For a long time, I was too afraid to meet new people, so I told myself I was "content to be shy." Soon, it started to get to me. As you get older, it becomes more and more important to make contacts. People have an amazing diversity in talents, and if you know more people, you'll have more resources to pool. For example, during my time as a reporter for the school newspaper, I often conducted original research. Knowing my classmates helped me find the ideal person to interview for a story.

Find your sweet spot in one of the activities offered at school, and you'll be well on your way to becoming a more outgoing person.

The best way to overcome shyness is to get involved. In particular, theater and debate changed the way I interact with people. Participation in plays allowed me to meet a huge number of people, and the experience of performing on stage helped me gain confidence in front of crowds. Both can do wonders for your public speaking ability. But if these aren't your cup of tea there are many other activities to get involved in. Find your sweet spot in one of the dozens of activities offered at school, and you'll be well on your way to becoming a more outgoing person.

Dr. Wes: John's got it going on here. What he didn't mention is just how common this problem is among teenagers. I just dealt with it this morning and several times over the previous week. Shyness, or "social anxiety" as we call it in psychobabble, appears in childhood and continues into adulthood, but rarely is it more of a problem than in adolescence. This is because teens need to be social to get along on a daily basis at school, work, and play. As John notes, even introverted teens need some small set of social connections to feel good about themselves and validated on their place and future in the world.

Some elements of shyness involve a self-perception of awkwardness and incompetence in social relationships. Unfortunately, this creates a downward spiral as the shy person avoids getting involved with anyone. As a shy girl put it to me just the other day, "I feel like I'm intruding on other people." No amount of talking someone out of this perception seems to work. Friends and family may express great adoration, but the shy person can't accept that information as real. It just doesn't make sense to them.

As the shy person pulls back, others get frustrated or feel alienated from them. They are seen as "aloof" or distant rather than just awkward. This, in turn, makes others feel uncomfortable, which causes them to perceive the shy person as socially incompetent. This makes the shy person feel worse, and (you guessed it) they respond by feeling more awkward and incompetent.

Some shy or awkward kids are absolutely certain others are talking about them in a negative way. Of course, in middle and high school, that's probably true, which only further energizes their fears. In fact, the difference between these kids and everyone else seems to be in how much they really care. The shy ones worry deeply about social interactions, while more confident ones blow off little slights or mistakes.

At its worst, social anxiety is treated with medication. This may sound like a mighty drastic solution to a common problem, but when you're worrying so much about these issues that you can't go to school or you get physically ill, it's time to nail the problem. The longer it goes on, the harder it is to deal with, leaving young adults feeling each day almost as rattled and nervous as they did on the first morning of seventh grade. For less serious cases, family and individual therapy are often sufficient to adjust problematic thought patterns in both teens and parents.

The reality is that one's *feelings* of shyness won't change. They are a part of who we are and how we respond to the world. What we can change is how we think about those feelings and how we choose to respond or not respond to them.

Sleepover Dilemma

Dear Dr. Wes and Marissa,

I'm a junior high girl and I'm having a sleepover. I didn't invite someone I see all the time. How do I handle it?

Marissa Ballard: I'd first want to know why you didn't invite her. You say that you see her all of the time, but aren't the two of you friends? If not, then she probably will not think anything of it. If you are friends, she is inevitably going to feel hurt and left out. The only thing you can do is be honest and prepared to offer an apology or good explanation as to why you excluded her. It's important that you be as kind as possible when you talk to her and try not to be surprised if she is angry and doesn't want to speak to you at all.

At every point in our journey to adulthood, we face these kinds of dilemmas. If we listen, they teach us a lot about how to get along with others.

Friends are likely to have fights when something like this happens because it's embarrassing for the person who wasn't invited. Think how you would feel if you learned that the majority of your friends were doing something together, but they left you out.

Try to make it up to her. Set aside a time when the just the two of you can spend some time together and hopefully patch up any rough spots in your friendship. This could be a sleepover or simply hanging out for a few hours after school.

From now on, when you're having a party or sleepover that excludes some of your friends, don't talk about it in front of others. Learning to tactfully handle situations like this can help you avoid more awkward moments in the future.

Dr. Wes: I think there's a larger issue here. At every point in our journey to adulthood, we face these kinds of dilemmas. If we listen, they teach us a lot about how to get along with others. Among the toughest of these struggles is learning to think more about others and less about yourself; to consider how you impact the world with your actions. Teenagers are terrific at identifying how every little thing—parents, school, gas prices, friends—improves or messes up their lives. They have a lot harder time understanding how their actions influence others. In fact, many kids feel pretty weak and unimportant, so they tend to miss all the damage (or good) they can do every day. Others have been treated badly at home or in school and simply don't care whom they hurt.

A person of any age has a responsibility to think about how they are treating others and to act ethically; to think about and do what is right for ourselves, others and our world. Whether you realize it or not, your question really asks us, "What's the ethical thing to do here?"

If this girl believes she should be invited and will feel left out if she's not, then the question is whether it is unethical to not invite her. If her feelings will be hurt because she is a friend and expects to be asked, then Marissa is on the money. You owe her an apology. However, if she is not such a good friend, there is something wrong with your communication which has caused her to see herself as a candidate for your sleepover, and thus left out.

An easy answer is to reach out and draw her in. However, you can't be friends with everyone and your parents aren't going to host a sleepover for 300 girls. So, what's important here is to be clear where she stands with you and to be kind and respectful if you exclude her. Whether you believe in the Golden Rule, karma, or some other philosophy, a fundamental principle of social interaction is to factor into all your choices the feelings and needs of others.

Failure to do so will ultimately return to haunt you. When was the last time you saw a teen movie where the mean girls won out in the end?

Mean Girls

Dr. Wes: I recently attended the play *The Secret Life of Girls* with my ten-year-old daughter. It featured a talented cast of teens[10] taking a serious look at the "mean girls" phenomenon.

Bullying is nothing new, but this play effectively illustrates how peer mistreatment has advanced in the last few years. The characters use technology including cell phones, instant messenger accounts, and online postings to reinforce constantly changing alignments and estrangements among their social group. They wield rumors, manipulations, condescension, and exclusion like surgical instruments to carve out what little self-esteem their peers might have, with devastating results.

Even more disturbing was the play's emphasis on how easy it is to go from victim to offender, as roles shifted, alliances formed, and various girls were included or exiled from the group. In watching the story unfold, it became clear how desperate and fearful each teen was of being the odd girl out, leading her to gratefully trade in the outcast status for that of the bully.

During the discussion afterward, several audience members recalled their own difficult days as teenagers. For some, those days came last week; for others, thirty years ago. But few seemed surprised at what they saw on stage. The play was realistic, and careful to raise more questions than it answered, leaving us to finish the storyline in our own families, schools, and communities.

Bullying is like the flu; it adapts to new generations and technology in the blink of an eye.

Some believe meanness among teens is simply a part of growing up and that a certain hierarchy will naturally emerge. Like *Lord of the Flies,* you will fill any vacancy of structure with your worst characteristics. I, instead see bullying as a process of social learning, and we cannot expect more of you as teenagers than we do of ourselves as adults. You go where we send you.

I once worked in an agency where one person spread false rumors about how others were having affairs or being sanctioned by licensure

---

[10] Both Kelly Kelin and Samantha Schwartz were featured in this play (written by Linda Daugherty), before winning the contest and signing on as back-to-back co-authors of Double Take.

boards. In one case, this person claimed that another staff member had to leave the agency because of a secret pregnancy with another staffer— a total load of bull. This gossipmonger was a therapist and a parent, yet saw nothing wrong with carrying on a horrific and destructive behavior that led to numerous resignations.

Take a look at the various blog entries and comments across the country and locally. You'll see adults spreading nasty, hateful comments about community members or political figures just as often as they engage in intelligent and reasonable discussion. Most of it is anonymous, so nobody has to take personal responsibility for anything they say. So, why would we expect teens to act differently?

It's easier to comfort someone who is a victim of hate than to confront the person who perpetrates it. Yet, both are important in helping you live peacefully with one another.

Julia Davidson: Bullying is like the flu; it adapts to new generations and technology in the blink of an eye. Only in the past few years has the reality of girls as bullies been brought to light. Female bullying does psychological damage to another person without laying a finger on them. Unfortunately, there are no mental Band-Aids to heal the injuries bullying girls can inflict on one another, and those wounds can last longer and be more harmful than the typical schoolyard fight.

As bullying has evolved, there are some new strains to look for among girls. There is of course the "insult-you-to-your-face" method as well as the "gossip-behind-your-back" technique. But it can also include more subtle and indirect approaches, including purposefully ignoring or excluding someone. Girls are known for separating into cliques, and when someone they don't know or don't like pulls them out of that comfort zone, having the power to disregard that person's existence feels pretty good. Those groups discover both power in their numbers and the means to abuse that power for amusement or sport. Many younger girls, no matter how quiet or haughty, only want to be included and liked. It's not for me to say who should be friends with whom, but selectively making and breaking friendships, or excluding someone "just because" isn't funny or justifiable. It's just plain mean.

Nowadays, cliques have faded and taking their place are alliances, the complexities and scopes of which are mindboggling. It would take volumes to describe the hierarchies of teenaged female friendships—the acquaintances, the friends, the person one calls her "best friend," and the real best friend. And, as Wes notes, girls are willing to align themselves with friends against other friends. At any given moment, a girl could side with Friend-A against Friend-B but with Friend-B against Friend-C, leaving many unsure who their true friends are at any given moment. This isn't direct bullying but it certainly enables and incites a girl to relish cattiness and hurtful gossip.

The final form of bullying is that fine-tuned ability of girls to nitpick someone to tears. It's the reason why we're so easily jealous, self-conscious, and willing to nitpick back. Today, such spiteful behavior can take place via text message or on Facebook, or it can slip into everyday conversation as an insult disguised as a joke. It takes its toll by slowly wearing away at the target, making her feel inclined to pick apart others to make the bullying stop.

Unfortunately, bullying is always renewing itself and isn't going to stop anytime soon. Counteracting it among girls requires tolerance and empathy, which few are able to demonstrate at this age, because it goes so far against the norm.

8 TEEN TECH

Facebook Eats the World

Dr. Wes: A few weeks ago, I sat in my office eating lunch and responding to email, when I realized that all four of my morning clients had discussed problems related to Facebook. I'm cloaking all confidential details, but one woman lost her husband to somebody he'd met on Facebook; a teen admitted her grades were dropping because she was seriously addicted to Facebook FarmVille. Another person felt her spouse was too flirtatious while online. After lunch, this trend continued. A college girl's best friend had, purely as a joke, gotten on her Facebook when she was away and changed her status to "Going into Rehab." It stuck for several hours before the girl caught it. She was not amused, nor was her family. Her minister called to say that he was praying for her.

Facebook is just a tool. You can use a hammer to drive a nail or hit yourself in the forehead with it.

This went on throughout the day until seven out of eight clients had shared a Facebook-related problem. I finally asked my last clients of the day if they too had come to talk about Facebook. The couple looked at each other and said, "No, but we could if you want to. We've got issues there, too."

On my drive home, NPR said that *The Social Network* had a good shot of winning "Best Picture" at the Oscars. Later, the news anchor described how Facebook was an essential element in the unrest in

Egypt. That night I had a dream about Facebook. It had eaten the world. Okay. I made that part up, but the rest is true, even if I scrambled the stories to protect confidentiality.

I asked the college girl whether her rumored trip to rehab didn't justify signing off Facebook forever. She looked at me with great wisdom in her eyes and shook her head. "No," she said. "You have to understand that Facebook is just a tool. You can use a hammer to drive a nail or hit yourself in the forehead with it."

Good point. But after hearing each of these stories and a hundred others, I've reached one conclusion: Our online power has greatly exceeded our ethics and nowhere is that truer than on Facebook, where anyone, of any age, has his or her very own newspaper with world-wide distribution and zero editorial control. So, my advice this week is simple: Think before you click. As the circumstances in Egypt confirm, we common folk have never held in our hands (and track pads) anything close to the power of Facebook. Now would be a good time to reflect on how to use it.

Aim for the nail, not the forehead.

Ben Markley: Social networking. Does it bring us closer or push us apart? People can't seem to agree, but we do know one thing: it's not an adequate replacement for actual relationships.

In the real world, there isn't a button I can click to create or accept a friendship, and relationships are tricky and complex. They can even be awkward or burdensome. Our close friends are often our harshest critics as well as our greatest supporters. Facebook is a great way to stay in touch. It's also a great way to waste time and avoid real life relationships and communication.

It should be seen as a compliment to socializing, not the stuff itself. Scissors are great for cutting paper, but you can't cut down trees with them. Facebook isn't a bad thing. We just need to use it the right way, for the right reasons.

Too Many Filters?

Dear Dr. Wes and Kelly,

I'm fifteen and my parents still restrict me from using the Internet without filters. I might be okay with that if they were filtering out porn or something bad, but they don't let me access Facebook, MySpace, or anything else that everybody uses. Don't you think this is pretty extreme? It's making it so I don't even want anything to do with them anymore. Maybe they'll listen to you.

Dr. Wes: In the old days, you had to go to the bad neighborhood or dial the bad telephone number to see or hear bad things. You had to travel into the big bad city to involve yourself in big bad happenings. You had to know bad people with bad ideas to be really, *really* bad. With the Internet, one has to exert about .05 calories worth of energy to click from reruns of *Mr. Roger's Neighborhood* to pretty much anything you can imagine and a great deal you could not.

It sounds like your parents are quite aware of this and have decided to increase the level of effort it takes to go to the bad neighborhoods of the Internet, which is

And there you are, caught in that one moment in time...forever.

about all they can hope for. The problem for you is that their view of what's negative in cyberspace exceeds yours and includes social networking sites. What you didn't tell us is what exactly they're concerned about: cyber-bullying, posting of inappropriate content, addiction to massive multiplayer games? You really have to try and walk a mile or two in their shoes and understand what they're afraid of before asking them to change the policy.

My favorite problem right now is the Internet's perfect memory. You might decide after a few weeks that those cool pictures of you and your buds acting up in your boxers aren't as great an idea as you thought. So, you take them down. Too late. The images still live out there on various servers, cut and pasted to other people's hard drives. And there you are, caught in that one moment in time...forever. Just try out the Wayback Machine some time to see how everything is archived online. Clever employers are even searching the blogs and web pages of applicants now, getting to know them better than they might like. Not what you were expecting when you signed up, huh?

If your parents are concerned about this kind of blowback, you should sit down and propose some rules and limits on private postings that might manage their anxiety. Maybe their fears aren't justified, but in order to resolve a problem or disagreement with anyone, you first have to understand them, and then work to meet them where they're at.

Kelly Kelin: Whether parents like it or not, teens are constantly keeping up with the latest fads. Whether it's the latest version of the iPod, the newest cellular device, or the fastest growing social network, kids will get caught up in the big trends. It's only natural that parents want to provide the best for you by showing and teaching you responsibility.

Facebook is highly overrated. Yes, it may be an easy, effective way to stay in touch with friends, but many of us have become obsessed with it. Too often, I see my peers rushing to the next available computer to either check or update their status. It's become such a habit that the school district has blocked these sites from its computers. On the other hand, as much as your parents would like to shelter you from all the pitfalls of society, you will still face them one day.

I know at fifteen it seems unfair, but not being allowed a Facebook or MySpace account isn't going to make much of a difference in your life. Your parents are just trying to do what they feel is best for you.

Electronic Relationships

Samantha Schwartz: With cell phones, email, instant messaging, and social networking sites, there are perhaps too many ways for couples to be in contact. Using all this technology is like baking cookies, all the ingredients need to be in balance. While there are thousands of combinations that would make a good cookie, the relationship of the ingredients to each other is what makes a recipe so delicious. I hope these suggestions are helpful in keeping your relationship tasty (and tasteful):

- Don't text, email, or instant-message about any topic that might carry emotion. Remember the "call" button on your phone? It allows you to address problems in an interactive way. Better yet, address your problems in person. Also, avoid texting just to say "What's up?" which implies that you need to know what the other person is up to all the time and vice versa. Such hounding is unhealthy.

- If your partner is an avid texter, setting boundaries may mean she will now text someone else more than you. If this makes you uncomfortable, be honest about your feelings. Have an in-depth talk about whom you text and how often.

- Talk about whether you and your partner are allowed to go through each other's phones. You could let each other look at pictures or texts whenever you want. It doesn't mean you lack trust. It means you just don't have anything to hide. However, this isn't for everyone. If you opt out, be sure each of you is completely comfortable with what you won't know about each other's lives. Constantly asking to see your phone is a sign of a controlling person, but if your partner always keeps his phone away from you, he obviously has something to hide. In either case, you both need to have a talk.

- If you both have a Facebook or MySpace account, decide whether you want to be listed as "In a Relationship." I recommend not, because everyone will instantly know when your breakup occurs, which is almost as bad as proclaiming the end of your relationship on the morning announcements at school. However, leaving your status as "Single" sends the wrong message. Instead, remove your relationship status from your profile completely.

- Discuss whether to share passwords. I recommend you don't, because if you break up, you could be in serious trouble before you can change all the codes. Instead, be open with each other about whom you talk to online.

- Try not to stalk the other person's page. Force yourself only to check once per week. Checking more often will make you seem crazy and may even make you feel that way.

Don't fail to set these boundaries just because you fear your partner will find it unattractive. You may be surprised at the appreciation you garner for making your needs clear. Chances are, if you're dating the right person, talking about these issues will bring you closer.

Dr. Wes: Rules? Guidelines? Limits? Meaningful dialog? My, how the world has gotten complicated for teenagers. But Samantha is right. As we've discussed in the years since Double Take got its first ink, technology usually runs faster than the guardian angel of good sense can fly, and we've given some pretty accurate forecasts of where things were headed. So, the idea of having specific rules of engagement for these technologies is always a welcome topic.

Don't get me wrong. I love technology. An earlier version of my first computer is now on display at the Smithsonian. I had a Mac in 1988. I have a smartphone. I'm a Webmaster. I get thirty texts a day, which I used to think was a lot. But I'm increasingly worried about the way in which teenagers are so completely tuned into these technologies. It's not so much that you lack real-world friends. Online friends are real, too. What I'm concerned about is the constant demand of Facebook and, more keenly, cell phones and text messaging, as if we really needed to be connected 24/7. I know kids (and so do you) who wake up routinely at night to text their friends. You text from class, and even while driving (please stop!).

The core issue is nothing new. By design, you are creatures of networking. We've just given you new ways to make that happen in a hyper-manic, never-ending stream. I have this fantasy—actually it's an inevitability, given how things are going—that before I die, people will have this chip in their brain and they'll just have to think "Suzie, what are you doing Friday?" and Suzie's chip will hear that and she'll say, "Let's go to the virtual reality show at the mall." I don't know whether my fantasy nightmare will ever happen, but we'd better have some clearer guidelines of how to interact—along the lines of what Samantha suggests—long before it does.

Otherwise, by the time you hit thirty, we're going to be a nation of people who need anxiety medication just to cope with the stress of our own inventions.

Texting Etiquette

Samantha Schwartz: Texting is fast, easy and fun. Even my parents (for God sake) have turned into texting pros. But when it comes to having serious conversations, texting is about as useful as a lawn gnome, and it can be twice as ugly.

Tone of voice cannot be conveyed in a text message, so it's easy to interpret someone else's words as rude or hostile. This can easily escalate into fights as each of the texters tries to think of clever and, eventually, vicious comebacks. Emoticons can help set the mood of a text and "jk" (just kidding) can indicate the comedic/sarcastic tone of your comments, but don't assume such symbols automatically make your intentions clear. You may still offend the other person.

Response time is equally unreliable. It's impossible to know whether the person you're texting hasn't responded because she doesn't want to, was offended, or is just busy. Was your message somehow lost or slowed-down in the air between your phone and hers? As time passes, the uncertainty and worry mounts. If the topic you wanted to discuss was so important that it now has you panicked, you should have waited to discuss it in person.

One advantage of texting is that you have time to think about your response. However, because of this, people take texts more seriously. On more than one occasion, even after carefully thinking through what I wanted to say, I ended up regretting a text about a second after I sent it. A text makes a concrete, visual, potentially permanent statement. Anyone can show your friends every word of your serious conversation or argument, without being shown the context in which you made what seems like a mean or insensitive comment.

Sam and I aren't the only ones capable of such fame. All you have to do is hit "send" and your message can be a matter of public record too.

I'm just as guilty as the next person when it comes to trying to have important conversations via text. But I'm tired of feeling text regret. Next time, I'll take my own advice and pick up the phone or go meet the person face-to-face.

Dr. Wes: Samantha's words are true—and printed right here in Double Take every week for everyone to see. Are you so brave? Would you want to have all your personal comments published and then reprinted worldwide on websites everywhere, right there with your name? Sam and I aren't the only ones capable of such fame. All you have to do is hit "send" and your message can be a matter of public record too. Forever.

Maybe you've never thought of it that way before, but that's what you do every time you post a message. If it goes up on your phone or Facebook or any other electronic media, you've authored your very own opinion column. Throw in a juicy fight with your boyfriend, or a couple of sexy pictures, and you may reach a wide audience you never knew was interested in your work.

Like Sam, I text a lot, and the kids and parents with whom I work appreciate the accessibility of communicating with me that way. I like it because I can choose when to respond and it leaves a record of our discussions. But the minute things get serious or emotional, I hit "call back." When communication is critical, there's no substitute for a voice or, better yet, a face. Still, I see kids starting relationships, living them out and then ending them all by text messaging.

Sure, that's a great way for shy persons to get up and do what needs to be done, and it does offer a chance to think things through—if you use it. But these online discussions can easily get botched up. I've spent entire sessions trying to help teenagers figure out how to undo text message misunderstandings, mistakes, and miscues.

But wait. Before you let your parents rush out and shut down the unlimited free texting, let's try and learn to use these devices correctly, not avoid them. Texting is here to stay, though hopefully not quite the way we're seeing it now. It is a vital part of teen culture and its virtues do outweigh its evils.

Some standards for texting are obvious: Not while driving. Not after 10 p.m. No sext messages or hot pix. Others are subtler, such as not fighting with friends, no threats, and no bullying.

Bottom line: Most good things have a dark side. Let's try and keep the lights turned on with this one.

Sexting Pix: Part 1

Dr. Wes: Several years ago we began running periodic columns about sexting,[11] before we even knew that was what it would be called. Over the years, the problem has only grown and, of late, it's appearing with astounding frequency.

The research tells us that teens have little to fear from "online predators" and a lot to fear from what you yourselves put out into cyberspace. Those cool digital cameras, phones and webcams produce pictures that no longer need a developer, so you're free to explore just about anything your eyes can see and commit it to a microchip.

All adults did foolish things as teens. Today those behaviors can be captured and kept forever in brilliant color.

Words fail me in describing what a bad idea this is. Storing sexually explicit images of anyone under the age of eighteen (including yourself), on a phone, computer, or other digital device is committing an act of child

---

[11] The first of these is found in Chapter 8 of *Dear Dr. Wes...Real Life Advice for Parents of Teens* under the title "Naked Pictures."

pornography. If you're underage in your state, any explicit acts depicted may be used as evidence of a sex offense.

Worse (if that were even possible), digital images copy from one device to another in a couple of seconds and the impact of "viral video" across the web is well-known. You may think your boyfriend is the only recipient of that special intimate picture, and that might be true. For now. But once you break up there's no telling what may happen to the image. And we all know how much kids love to get into each other's phones, so that once-secure image may be easily found and forwarded to everyone.

I'm astounded at how many upstanding young people who get into no other kinds of trouble are finding the irresistible urge to do this. All adults did foolish things as teens, including your parents and me. The problem is that today those behaviors can be captured and kept forever in brilliant color.

Think before you point and shoot.

Ben Markley: True, sexting won't impregnate anyone, but the concept behind it reminds me of the annoying kid we all sat by in 3rd Grade who would put his finger right where you could feel it on the tips of your hair and say, "I'm not touching you!"

Whatever the convenience of "not touching" someone's virginity, there's something to be said for the cheapening nature of it all. Those who spend all their time fantasizing about perfect Hollywood sex are going to be disappointed when the real deal comes along. They might find themselves actually preferring their ripoff to the real deal, and then what's the point?

Sex is a big enough issue as it is. Getting your phone involved borders on the ludicrous.

Sexting Pix: Part 2

Dr. Wes: Last week we discussed the sexting revolution, especially as it includes sexually explicit digital photography. If it's too late and those images already exist, here's how to avoid making a bad situation worse.

- Never transmit those images between devices. You may think they're going to just one person, but that violates the whole point of digital information. Assume the worst.

- Store all media containing explicit photos of yourself in a secure place. If you're a minor, it is illegal to share them. If you destroy them, do so with certainty. When we "delete" a file we're just pushing it out of the directory. Even an entry level geek can work around that.
- *Never ever* carry sexually explicit images on your phone. This is begging for a breach of privacy and potential legal charges.
- If some other minor is depicted in those images, destroy the material right this minute. No ifs, ands, or buts. Take the phone in and ask your cell phone provider to reset the phone to factory settings and completely erase the storage card and to make a note of having done so on your account. That way if you are accused and your phone is taken and analyzed you can point out that you did your best to eliminate the illegal images. Same goes for computers or camera chips.
- If an image is sent to your phone before you know what hit you, find out at once how to purge it.

If you're hell-bent on ignoring this advice and you get caught, be aware of your Miranda rights. Think of *Law and Order*. "You have the right to remain silent." Your phone or computer is your property. Never give it up to anyone without a warrant. While phones may be confiscated at school when they are being used improperly, schools do not have a right to access the data on your devices.

If you're asked to provide an unlocking code (and you better have a really good one), don't do it and contact your parents immediately. At that point, they should seek the advice of an attorney before relinquishing the codes or phone. The attorney can advise you on reasonable search and seizure and probable cause. We all have a legal right to due process. Learn everything there is to know about yours before you need it.

What may seem fun in one context can turn illegal down the road, and nowhere is that a steeper slope than in the area of sexting and sexual photography.

Ben Markley: Maybe this all sounds a little over your head. With all the sexual drama we see among teenagers on TV and all the rumors we hear at school about hookups, all this sex-tech stuff would seem to have no consequence. I mean, you're not really having sex with anyone, right?

Yeah sure, but if you and/or the other person are under eighteen, you're stepping into the realm of child pornography. Send it, you get charged with production; keep it, you get charged with possession. Not exactly a fun fact you want buzzing in the halls at school or on your permanent record.

Privacy is sketchy in light of social networking. Your phone is not safe. The instant it receives or sends a "sext," you start carrying a huge chunk of incriminating evidence in your pocket. Your friends may think it's funny. A judge won't.

Google these cases. We're not kidding about this.

9 FAMILY LIFE

Younger Siblings

Samantha Schwartz: As I get closer to leaving for college, I think more about what it will be like for my little sister in a few months. She says that even though I won't be around, she'll still think of me in the first weeks of every school year, when teachers mistake her for me. In earlier grades, teachers called her Samantha by accident all the time; one even gave up and just called her "Little Samantha," much to her dismay. Apparently, they expected her to be exactly like me and she's worried about disappointing them.

As the oldest child in my family, I never experienced older sibling comparisons. I've always been free to pave my own way and make my own impressions. I can't imagine what it would be like to have teachers expect things of me before I even enter their classrooms.

Younger siblings need interests and activities that are uniquely their own. At the same time, parents shouldn't pressure the younger ones to be different just for the sake of being different. My sister and I both sing and act. We both love to write and are both interested in journalism. Since she was eight, however, my sister has been writing short stories and plays for the fun of it, and recently started acting in community theater. I never did that. There, the director knows her and only her, and she gets to have a fresh start.

Finally, encourage your younger sibs to develop their own views about things. Make it clear that they don't have to value and appreciate everything you do or how you see the world. My sister came along on most of my college tours and, although she groaned about it, she learned something important—while we're similar in some important ways, the colleges that appealed most to me sickened her more than peanut butter on fried eggs.

To an older sibling like me, being the younger one looks pretty tough, but, with careful parenting, I think my sister and her younger sibling peers will be just fine.

Dr. Wes: Actually, peanut butter is really pretty good on everything. Otherwise, I'm with Sam. You'd think the vast differences between teens are a little less apparent within a given sibling set. But I've seen families with three or four kids who all seem to have grown up in different foreign countries—or planets.

There are about a hundred ways to categorize kids, so it's dangerous even to get started. But we all crave labels, whether we admit it or not, so I'll offer a couple to toss around.

I think of most kids as being somewhere on a scale between caring too much on one end or caring too little on the other. I don't mean morally—like they just don't care about the environment or other people. I just mean they don't notice or respond to what goes on around them. The farther you lean in this direction, the more you tend toward attention deficit. The farther you lean toward caring too much, the more likely you are to have problems with anxiety.

> *Most discipline problems come from a mismatch between parenting style and kid personality.*

Now, before readers run to their word processors, I'm not proposing that you all need to be diagnosed and treated for one thing or the other. Quite the opposite. By understanding how you "lean," you can help your parents figure out how to parent you. For example, care-too-much kids work harder with less stress applied. In fact, if parents press them too hard the kid produces less, or even worse, gets overwhelmed. Care-too-little kids need more rewards, guidelines, and structure. They have to be pushed or they won't get much done.

Sibling sets sometimes include kids who lean in opposite directions and thus need different approaches, whereas parents prefer a one-size-fits all approach. Yet, just as Sam notes, what worked with you can easily fall flat with your brother or sister.

Understanding which way you lean can help you train your folks to do more of what works with you and less of what doesn't. While that seems like a real "duh" concept, most discipline problems come from a mismatch between parenting style and kid personality. It may take some work, but if you give your parents a hand, they'll learn to do what Samantha proposes—offer each sibling a unique experience of being a singular member of your family.

Loser?

Dear Dr. Wes and Marissa,

I am a fifteen-year-old boy who has lost nearly everything. I made some pretty serious mistakes with school and drugs. I caused my family so much pain and embarrassment, including extra financial stress because of legal issues. I lost friends, the respect of my teachers, and the trust of my family. What bothers me most is that no one will trust me. I don't want to be labeled a loser. Other than moving away to get a fresh start, what can I do to win back their trust? I want to make it right.

Dr. Wes: You've faced a lot of struggles for a young man of fifteen and I appreciate your desire to make amends. To do so, however, you must first give up what you want most: Winning back anyone's trust or receiving their forgiveness. Teenagers are for loving, liberating, protecting, teaching, growing, valuing, etc. They're not for trusting—your experiences provide a good example of why.

Your family is disappointed and feels let down by your behavior. Their anger and pain are only made worse by their view that you violated their most fundamental faith in you. That feeling of betrayal, which is clear in your letter, means that they trusted you to behave a certain way and, instead, you acted another. Expecting trustworthiness among teens often leads parents to over-personalize their behavior, which in turn produces hostility and resentment. I actually hope your parents will decide *not* to be so trusting in the future. That will allow them to keep better track of you and your bad choices, and to react before things get out of hand. You should see this not as a burden but as very liberating, as it gives you a chance to fail and be redirected, rather than feeling like a failure as a person.

In starting over, you will stumble. I guarantee it. But if each slip up only offers your family a renewed sense of betrayal, you'll actually fall deeper and deeper in the hole, the more you try to get out. While your path back to respectability may be a long one, it's pretty clearly marked. You must first get involved in some kind of treatment. One of the best is still Alcoholic's (or Narcotic's) Anonymous. There are other programs including Rational Recovery and SMART. If you think your issues are really not based on addiction, but just bad choices in life, then you might start with therapy and let the therapist help decide what will work best for you. By regularly attending and working on recovery, therapy or both, you can show that you're genuinely trying to change.

Next, get a job and contribute whatever you can to your legal and treatment expenses. In our clinic, we call this "reparation" because it helps repair the damage you've done to your relationships with others. Develop a plan to make amends to those you've harmed by sharing with your family and friends the sadness you feel for having made poor decisions.

If you continue to hold yourself to higher standards, people will witness changes, and begin to accept them.

You're not a loser, but you must take a position of humility without being humiliated. Be humble, admit your mistakes, and put forth a good faith effort to change. Trust and forgiveness will come when the relationship is repaired and you're more developmentally ready to handle it, but now is a good time to start earning back both.

Marissa Ballard: Every teen comes to a point in his (or her) life where he feels he's let everyone down and no one trusts him anymore. Of course, the individual circumstances vary in type and degree, but you're not alone in your feelings of frustration.

Regaining someone's trust is one of the hardest things to do. Unlike Wes, I do not think it's a bad idea to trust teens. In fact, it's extremely important. A teen needs to feel trusted or else it is hard to be motivated in life and in relationships. It also teaches him what "trust" really means and how easy it is to break someone's trust. Having said that, gaining it back will not be an easy feat for you.

When parents are disappointed and their trust is violated, it takes a long time and a lot of talking, patience and understanding, on everyone's part to build it back up. You will have to prove time and time again that you are changing. Even though you will probably feel frustrated in the process, remind yourself that you were the one who messed up in the first place.

It's wonderful that you want to start over and change yourself. You're only fifteen and you have plenty of time to do so. It will take a while for your friends, family, and teachers to get used to the new you, but eventually they will. If you continue to hold yourself to higher standards, people will witness your long-lasting behavioral and personality changes, and slowly begin to accept them.

Headed for Divorce

Dear Dr. Wes and Julia,

My family isn't that good for each other and we might get a divorce. Is there anything else we can try?

Julia Davidson: One Christmas, when I was younger, I witnessed my parents arguing over fruit salad. I'd never seen them argue like this and my most immediate fear was divorce. Most kids fear losing the security of the family they know now or knew when they were younger. Any hint of tension can cause you to assume the worst.

First, assess your situation thoroughly, looking not just at your parents' actions but at anything that could affect your family as well. Are there outside forces affecting your daily lives? Do your parents fight a lot? Stressed people tend to problem-solve in raised voices. When money becomes especially tight, their tolerance gets stretched to its limit. All families experience rough patches—my family's sore spot happened to be fruit salad. Some of those rough patches can really prove whether or not the parents are capable of staying together.

Divorce is only one possible option. Your parents may consider it, but end up choosing not to follow through. If your family really is headed for divorce, however, the best thing to do is learn to cope. Parents rarely split up on account of their kids. In fact, they often stay together for the sake of the family. So, in no way should you think the divorce is your fault.

You don't have to try and find a silver lining in all this or act like nothing is wrong, but showing your parents that you can accept what is happening will decrease the overall tension and help clarify what's really going on. I truly hope your family is just going through a rough time, but if divorce is imminent, don't hesitate to let your parents know how you feel and ask them to help you take measures to get through a tough time.

Dr. Wes: I agree that finding out what's really going on is a good idea before leaping to any conclusions. Sometimes fruit salad is really just fruit salad. Unfortunately, the statistics support your worries. Well over half of American families with children will face divorce, either before the kids leave home or after.

Divorce is particularly difficult for teenagers. Just as you're trying to pull away from your family in an age-appropriate manner and focus on your own relationships and loves, boom: your family suddenly falls apart. It might seem easier if you're already away at college, but I find it's often just as hard for college kids to accept that the home they remember is no longer there for them at the moment they really need that "base camp." So, in short, divorce is never easy and I can understand why you'd hope for alternatives.

An obvious one is for your parents to see a therapist to determine what's wrong in their relationship and whether it can be fixed. Sadly, research suggests that feuding couples wait an average of six years too long to go to therapy and, instead, avoid dealing with their differences until an easy solution is much less likely. Parents can try and stick out the marriage until the kids are really out on their own. This only works, however, if the parents are very tolerant of each other and able to put aside their difficulties and focus on their kids. Unfortunately, staying married to someone just to parent kids often leads to a rather lonely and depressing life. People need to feel loved and be able to show romantic love to someone, so these arrangements usually cause more problems than they solve.

When it comes right down to it, you really are correct—some families just "aren't that good for each other." There are many complicated reasons for that, which, as Julia notes, rarely have anything to do with the kids. If your parents have really considered their options, they may be best off splitting up. At that point, the golden question is as simple as it is serious: Will they carefully consider the best interests of their children or just end up creating more conflict and anger along the way?

I've seen it go both ways, and I hope your parents will listen to me when I tell them to cling desperately to a path of *kindness* and *respect* in every aspect of their divorce. Some divorces work out well for everyone. Others sink the family into a deep quagmire of suffering that is only rivaled by child abuse or alcoholism. In fact, at their worst, psychologists often see vicious custody battles as a special kind of abuse.

Hopefully, your parents will make a good decision about how to proceed, even if that isn't the one you hoped for. If they decide to split up, I hope they'll do so with gentleness to each other and to you and your siblings.

If they hold to those principles, things will turn out okay.

Distant Brother

Dear Dr. Wes and Samantha,

My brother has become less caring and more distant from the family in recent years. Over spring break, I tried to get him to come with me to visit our mom who moved almost 200 miles away last August. He hasn't seen her since last Christmas. I feel bad for my mom because she tries to stay connected via texts, Facebook, phone, etc., but he just never responds. Everyone in my family has tried to get him to see her. He also refuses to spend time with the rest of us, and when he does, he argues and curses us over small things like haircuts and taking out the trash. How do I get him to stop avoiding our family and deal with his angry behavior?

Samantha Schwartz: It sounds like your family has tried to reach out to your brother, even after he's treated you badly. I suspect his attitude has little to do with you and more to do with other issues, and I hope you and the rest of your family do not take his withdrawal personally. Try finding out what's going on in his life without badgering or appearing intrusive. Be like a ballerina; tread lightly, but with purpose. Offer to meet him for lunch or arrange a phone call at his convenience, but set a specific time and date so he can't blow you off. Keep things casual at first to start building rapport and trust. Wait until the second or third lunch to bring up serious issues.

Your brother may be acting out unresolved conflicts with your mom.

If your brother refuses to communicate with you or share what's bothering him, consider carefully approaching his friends. They may have inside information that can help you discover what he's going through so you can help find some solutions. This might make him mad, but at least he will know you care.

If he's still unresponsive, you've done all you can possibly do. Let him know that you care about and love him, and that you will be there when he's ready to talk about whatever is bothering him. But also tell him that he's reached a point where, if he continues to treat you poorly when he visits, you won't be inviting him anymore. Let him know that he is at risk of harming important relationships with his family, and you really don't want that to happen. But make sure he knows that, as long as he treats you respectfully and kindly, he is always welcome.

Dr. Wes: I'm taking a very different tack here, not because I disagree with Sam's perspective, but because I want to broaden it. You left out two important details—your brother's age and why your mom lives 200 miles away. I'll try and work around that by making some assumptions based on your letter. First, that he is a late teen and free to decline visiting your mom, and second, that your mom did not just up and leave the family or divorce your dad and move. If I'm wrong on either point, then your whole family needs to head to the therapist, pronto—even if Mom only joins you on Skype.

Whether you like his behavior or not, your brother may be acting out unresolved conflicts with your mom, even if she had no choice but to move away, perhaps for work. It's a horrible decision to have to make and should be avoided if at all possible, but sometimes it's necessary in this age of economic recession. It should only be made after getting everyone else on board and acknowledging the impact it will have. Regardless, your brother strikes me as one angry guy and your family owes it to him to try and find out why.

Here's where age makes a difference. If he's under eighteen and living at home, he needs to either pull it together or be required to see a therapist to help him do so. Unless a parent has done something terribly unjust or grossly inadequate, a child is obligated to work toward reconciliation, just as is a parent. Even if he's a young adult, someone needs to clarify that obligation, and the family should put pressure— economic, emotional, logistical to force the issue. Your brother is entitled to his feelings and ways of seeing the world, but growing up means dealing with conflict, and he isn't. He's just creating it and, at this point, nobody seems to know why.

The family also has an obligation to see that every member coexists in a reasonably just environment. Obviously, not everything is "fair" in life. If your mom has to live 200 miles away, that's unfair to everyone including her. But the real question your brother may be facing is whether his best interests were taken into account in making that decision. If they were, then he needs to understand those circumstances and come to terms with them. If they weren't, then your family will be struggling for some time with your brother and his issues.

Homeless Teen

Dear Dr. Wes and Marissa,

I'm an eighteen-year-old high school student who has been in and out of trouble my whole life. I was adopted at age four and have put my family through hell. I've had a drug problem the last few years and was kicked out of the house for it last year. I went through rehab and then moved back in with my father. I've been a good student, earning a 3.2 GPA, and I participate in sports. A week ago, my father found some paraphernalia in my room, and I confessed to doing drugs more than once, hoping he'd understand my problem and somehow help. I misjudged his patience and he kicked me out. Last night I slept out in the cold with no food and I have nowhere else to go. I don't know what to do, where to go, or whether college is even an option now. Any suggestions would help. Thank you very much.

Dr. Wes: Where to begin? First of all, I understand the absolute anger and frustration your parents feel about living with a young man using drugs and the trouble such use brings. Who can blame them for feeling upset with you? However, that anger and disappointment has gotten out of control. It is one thing to "kick your kid" into rehab. It's another to be finished with him entirely and to let him sleep on the street. I also understand that a core tenet of AA and ALANON is letting the addict "hit bottom." I don't know whether that's what is intended here, but your schoolwork and attempt to find help suggest to me that you may not be the derelict they seem to feel you've become.

If your recovery is stalling, you need to get to NA or AA at once, and your family needs to help you without enabling your addiction. Regardless of what you have done as a teenager, you seem to be trying to pull it together now and I would encourage you not to give up at this critical moment. Readers should take heed, because you're not as far removed from the average teenager as some may think. Kids have easy access to drugs and alcohol, and this is a good example of how recreational substance use can quickly go bad.

You need the help of your family, the community, and most notably, your own inner courage—which is clearly showing through in this letter—to pull up, get an education, and make your life better.

I hope someone will take a stand for you.

Marissa Ballard: The situation you are in right now is very sad. Despite your mistakes, no one deserves to go through this. The major obstacle in finding a solution is that at eighteen you're an adult, and that makes services harder to find.

I went searching for homes and resources, and found a lot of dead ends. I would suggest that you visit with your high school counselor or social worker to see what options you have. If you're not okay with that, is there another teacher or adult in the community with whom you're comfortable? Ask around.

Not only do you need help finding shelter, but I'd really encourage you to try and stay sober. There are a few programs offered by the state and the Salvation Army to help you. I've read that younger people are often targets for theft in homeless shelters, so I would try to pursue other avenues before choosing that one.

Hopefully, your father will come around and understand that he is not helping you to stay on the right path by kicking you out of his house. I am not sure what your history is with him, but I am a firm believer that, through nearly anything, your family should stick by you. Try to get in touch with him and see whether you can make amends. If that's not possible, try to take pride in the fact that you have managed to pull your grades back up and participate in a school activity. You really are making strides in bettering yourself.

10 PARENT-TEEN CONFLICT

Overprotective

Dear Dr. Wes and Marissa,

My parents are incredibly overprotective and, in the back of their minds, they must think I'm out at parties every weekend getting stoned or boozing it up. In reality, I'm sitting at Pizza Shuttle at midnight asking for a curfew extension and the only thing I ever hear on the other line is "Twelve o'clock is your curfew and we're not changing it." As a senior in high school, I think my parents should give me a little room and know I'm not one of the "naughty girls" stumbling through the door at curfew. So, how do I get them off my back and on my side?

If you're as upstanding as you claim, your parents would do well to encourage you.

Dr. Wes: The fundamental dilemma of parenting is this: How much do I push my kid and how much do I hold her? In your case, the "pushing" involves structure and protection versus the "holding" of freedom and acceptance. Since you read the column, you know that I see this as having little to do with trust and more to do with protection from self-destruction. You argue that you're more likely to overdo the pizza than the Jack Daniels, and I say power to you. Some kids certainly are more self-destructive than others. Many, like you, have adopted some good values and attitudes towards themselves, and now feel punished because the very parents who instilled those virtues won't let go so they can practice them.

So, to some degree, I must go along with you and warn parents that a failure to reinforce those values with age-appropriate privileges may make well-behaved kids feel alienated. Worse, it may cause those good kids to say "what the hell…might as well live up to what they think of me." Of course, getting into trouble to prove your parents right is about as foolish as you can get, so try and avoid falling into that trap. But if you're as upstanding as you claim, your parents would do well to encourage you.

However, getting them to do this means you may have to agree to some verification. Your parents can't trust you blindly, no matter how good you are. That would be naïve. So, if they want evidence of good behavior and you want to create a magnificent impression of who you are, let them smell your breath or even suggest they breathalyze you. Call in when you're supposed to, and let them call you, as long as they aren't being too intrusive. You could even let them give you the good old UA once in a while. Snap a shot on your camera phone and send home time stamped pictures of Pizza Shuttle. If you're willing to demonstrate that kind of good judgment, then your parents should lighten up.

You're about to turn eighteen and presumably moving out next fall. Ask them to help you learn to function as a young adult within the protective system I suggest above, or any other legitimate system you can agree on as a family. This way, your parents can both hold and push you, and all of you can benefit.

Marissa Ballard: Your best shot would be to simply sit down and talk to your parents about your curfew and restrictions and about why you feel they're unfair. I would like to point out, though, that not everyone is as fortunate as you when it comes to curfew. There are plenty of seniors still adhering to a "before a.m." curfew, so if your endeavor fails, know that you are not alone.

Pick the right time to talk—not a busy night or after a rough day at work. Do not bring it up in the middle of another argument about something different. In my house, the standard location for a family meeting is the kitchen table. Everyone sits down and looks at each other and shares their concerns, ideas, and complaints. Try to remain calm, thus demonstrating your maturity.

Explain that you feel you have shown responsibility by following your curfew in the past, and that you think you deserve a more flexible one now. Come up with a time that is not extremely far from the one that you already have—maybe one or two a.m., tops. Don't ask for or expect to receive an answer right away. This may take some contemplation on your parents' part. If a week goes by without a decision, remind them of your request no more than once or twice a week.

When I note that my curfew has been the same since sophomore year (11:00 or 11:30 p.m.), my parents point out that after 11:00 p.m. there's not much to do that's appropriate for high school aged kids. Statistics show that the chance of an alcohol-related accident increases after midnight. Their reluctance to allow you to stay out later may not be about you. It could be solely due to the fact that they do not trust the other people out and about after midnight. You might want to consider how you will counter those arguments. I hope that this discussion goes well for you. If not, you only have one more year left before you go away to college.

In the end, I appreciate having parents who show how much they care about me, even though it can be annoying or inconvenient at times. I hear from friends who've already moved out that you actually end up missing someone waiting up for you.

Blamed for Everything

Dear Dr. Wes and John,

How do you deal with a parent who blames you for everything and doesn't own up to his or her own mistakes?!

Dr. Wes: First, you owe it to yourself to be certain your perceptions are accurate. I realize you've already reached a conclusion on that, but it's worth taking a step backwards and trying to assess the situation objectively. Adolescence is marked by upheaval as children move away from their parents (literally and emotionally) and on to adulthood. There is about a 100% chance of hitting rough spots along the way, and both parent and child are likely to blame and be blamed at one time or another. So, a second opinion may be in order before you let your view of your family stick.

For now, let's assume that things are just as you suggest. It would be really tempting to point this out to your parents with great frequency, but I'm sure you've tried that and know how well it works. The more you point out weaknesses the more your parents feel defensive and cite your backtalk or disrespect. Throw in something about them being hypocrites and the whole thing goes up in flames. Instead, it may be best to just accept that your folks are flawed people. They've made their mistakes and will continue to do so.

Being "blamed for everything" can be very demeaning and, in its extreme forms, emotionally abusive. If your objective assessment leads you in this direction, it would be wise to track down a therapist. Typically, I'd suggest family therapy to help your parents focus on areas in which you all excel and work with you on your collective shortcomings. In many cases, parents just feel fed up and don't know what to do. If the therapist can give them something helpful, they'll use it. What you should not do is use family therapy like a club to bang you're mom and dad over the head for all their faults.

If you can't reach a peace between you and your folks, become more focused on the one person you can change—yourself.

In extreme cases, however, family therapy may not solve the problem, or it might even make things worse, because your parents may not acknowledge the effect they're having on you, even when it's pointed out. If that's really the situation, it may be better to see the therapist alone and just work on your future, learning to look for rewards and self-esteem in your talents and larger life endeavors. I don't think this is the best answer, but if you can't reach a peace between you and your folks, the next best thing is to become more focused on the one person you can change—yourself.

I've seen it work many times.

John Murray: Remember one fact your parents have probably been spouting since infancy—you are the child and they are the parents. In a head-on collision, you will lose. So, while I'll discuss a few ways to increase your leverage, I agree with Wes. You're going to have to come to terms with the fact that they aren't angelic. After a few decades, you may actually find yourself supporting some of the decisions your parents made back in your teen years. But there will also be issues on which you still disagree, and you may choose to raise your children differently. I know a woman who was so disgusted by her parent's habitual lateness that it inspired her to be punctual as an adult. In all of her children's years in school, she was only late picking them up twice.

You can resolve to change your own behavior, but you cannot do much to improve your parents. Realizing this is an important step to maturity. There are, however, a few ways to encourage your parents to accept responsibility, but pick your battles wisely. Give in on small issues, then respectfully discuss your opinions on important ones. This way, you'll appear less argumentative, and they will be inclined to look at your side of the story.

Be quick to admit mistakes. When you apologize to others, they often feel obliged to admit their own errors. Since your parent is already jumping on your mistakes, you have nothing to lose by apologizing, if you can be sincere about it. Don't say, "I'm sorry you feel that way." That implies you're sorry for your parent's faults and will likely fan an angry fire.

Finally, you would do well to talk to your school counselor, nurse, or clergy. They're experienced listeners, and can help you with specific issues I can't address, especially if your parent's blaming becomes abusive.

Home For The Holidays

Dear Dr. Wes and Samantha,

I'm a freshman in college and I can't exactly live under my mother's rules when I'm at home. I'm coming to town this holiday, but I made plans to stay at a friend's house because she basically lives at her boyfriend's and is never there. I wanted to run this idea by you and see what you thought and how I should approach my family with this. If I'm living in my family's house, there will be a lot of fights about what I can do and who I can hang out with. That's not what I want. I want to have a good Christmas break but...

Samantha Schwartz: I understand your desire for freedom over break. However, this time of change in your life is even harder for your parents than it is for you. There's a hole in their lives that you used to fill. You've met new people and live a new life at college. Deciding not to stay at home over the holidays is a big choice, and your decision will be very upsetting to them. Make sure you're prepared to accept that.

You've come up with a plan to avoid arguments, but if you don't handle this issue carefully, you could end up with even more fights.

Be firm but sensitive in how you broach this issue with your parents. It will be their first opportunity to see how you've grown up. Respect their feelings, but if you present the decision as being up for debate, it can only turn into an argument. Explain that, while away at college, you've led an independent lifestyle and it would be difficult to go back to living at home right now. Don't say you will never stay with them again, but explain that just for this break, you're staying with a friend. Add that you enjoy spending time with them, but you need your own space and you see this as the best way to avoid conflict so that the holiday is peaceful and fun for the whole family. This will help prove that you're not just ditching them to party with friends. You've just matured.

If you're not already wondering what awaits you on the road ahead, now is the time to consider what it really means to be a grownup.

Your time with family will already be limited, so work on making every moment there count. Promise to come over to the house often, and invite each member out for some alone time. Spend the night on Christmas Eve and stay through Christmas Day. Whenever you're there, focus on your family and don't bring friends over unless your family asks to meet them. Show them that you've grown up by helping out with dishes, vacuuming or cooking. Doing this will demonstrate that you still want to spend big holidays with them and be a part of the family, while setting a boundary for the rest of the break.

Be aware, however, that if you expect your parents to help pay for your food or living expenses over break, or after you go back for college, they may assert input into your decision. If you do end up staying at home, make sure your actions demonstrate your maturity. Then, the next time you want to try this, they'll offer less resistance.

Dr. Wes: Welcome to adulthood. If you're not already wondering what awaits you on the road ahead, now is the time to consider what it really means to be a grownup.

Our society does all it can to stretch adolescence way past its expiration date. This means that young adults hang on to the core task of youth—differentiating from mom and dad—longer than necessary. As Sam notes, this may have a lot to do with finances. Research tells us that most young people require some financial support from their families until age twenty-five. So, don't burn any bridges. As long as your parents have influence over your purse strings, there will be a conflict of interest between your need to become your own person and their need to direct you where they think you should go.

Some of this is perfectly legit. Parents *shouldn't* spend money on things that harm or don't advance your future. However, they should be incredibly careful how far they take this strategy. I've seen some pretty ridiculous attempts to manipulate young adults with money, leading to years of resentment. In your case, I'd advise your parents to cover whatever expenses they would incur if you lived at home over break and let you find money for the rest. Then, follow Samantha's holiday plan to help your parents accept this as a normal part of growing up. I've seen it happen, but I would *never* advise parents to discontinue paying for college expenses just because you find holidays at home fraught with conflict.

That said, growing up and differentiating from your family involves something far greater than where you live and who pays the bill. It means considering the feelings of others. You can live in Bulgaria and be perfectly self-sufficient, but if you do not consider the impact of your choices on your family and others, you will still be a child. If you handle this as Samantha suggests, however, you will have accomplished another milestone in your life.

That doesn't mean your parents will be ready to do their part to help that process along. It just means that you will have countered their major objection. If instead, you let this situation turn into a battle of wills between you and your folks, then everyone will lose.

So, the ball is in your court. Play the game wisely.

Boyfriend Sleepover

Dear Dr. Wes and Julia,

My boyfriend asked me if it was ok with my mom if he could spend the night at my house. I was wondering whether it would be ok and appropriate for him to do so. I also wanted to know whether I could stay in the same room with him. Here are two things I thought about so that my mom might be more comfortable with it: We could keep my door open during the night while we're asleep. I have another bed, so maybe he or I could sleep on that. Can you think of anything else that we could do to make the situation more comfortable for my mom? If this isn't a good idea, then that's ok, but I wanted to ask your opinion.

Dr. Wes: If the issue were sex, then the answer would be pretty simple. At your age, there's no good argument for involving your mom in your sex life, except to give you good advice on safety and avoiding pregnancy. It's one thing to have an open and honest relationship on these issues. It's quite another to expect your mom to condone her daughter's sexual expression in her home. Parents may see this differently for the over-eighteen crowd, but even then it's really their call.

> *Most boys would not think to ask you to do this—most girls wouldn't consider it an option and most parents would just say "no."*

If we instead accept you at your word, that you just want to have a coed slumber party with your b.f., then the issue becomes one of propriety—defined as *"correctness, modesty, and good manners."* Unfortunately, that perspective doesn't boost your argument either. Your mom has a right to feel uncomfortable about this, simply because it doesn't fit with an accepted practice in our culture. It's easy to say that she shouldn't care what other people think, but most kids and adults do. If you and your mom become known as the family that allows boys to spend the night, people will fill in the gaps however they want, and that won't make you or your mom feel very good.

The other odd thing here is that most boys would not think to ask you to do this—most girls wouldn't consider it an option and most parents would just say "no." It's not surprising that your boyfriend would ask you to stay out late or sneak out with him. That's against the rules (I presume), but it at least fits within normal teen culture, because nearly every teen has been asked and most have done it. But to ask your mom to openly accept this arrangement just seems weird to me, and it raises red flags as to how this guy thinks and what kind of home he grew up in.

In fact, some pretty good dating advice for you at this juncture of your life is to give a lot of thought to how any boy you're interested in has been raised. This guy seems kind of sketchy.

Julia Davidson: You are very mature to think about your mom's feelings and come up with ideas for this situation. Even so, I'm not sure how well the idea will fly with her. Parents have trouble leaving two teenagers in a room alone together for any period of time, and often for good reason. Even if you take all of the right precautions, things can still happen (read: SEX) and result in untimely consequences (read: BABIES). The last thing parents want is their child making a mistake in the heat of the hormonally-charged moment and it being partially their fault for being too permissive.

For now, I'd say hold off on the sleepover and find an alternative. Ask your mom to consider a coed sleepover with a group of friends (b.f. included) and with a set of ground rules ahead of time about supervision. With a bigger group and a clear understanding of rules, the focus would be more on having fun and less about the intimacy of sleeping with someone.

Another option would be having your boyfriend stay late into the evening but not overnight. Think of activities that take the focus away from potential sex and on to more parent-friendly ideas, while still keeping an element of privacy to your relationship.

Tattoo You

Dear Dr. Wes and Julia,

What's your opinion on kids getting tattoos or body piercing under the age of eighteen? My mom is totally against it, even though she knows it's much more common now and not a sign that you are low class, or whatever. This is just a way I want to express myself, and I see this as her being controlling.

Dr. Wes: Including tattoos and body piercing in the same letter is kind of like comparing apples and monkeys. Tattoos are permanent and most piercings are not. No matter how sophisticated you are as a teenager, there's little chance you'll be the same person in ten years or twenty or thirty that you are now. Or, at least, I sure hope you won't.

Your brain will only finish developing in your mid-twenties, along with your adult personality, and by then you'll be exposed to many new influences. Your entire life will have changed, in fact, including whom you love, the career path you select, whether to have children, and so on. Little of this can be predicted now and all of it may influence what sort of body art you choose and how it reflects who you are over a lifetime. What I might have fancied at eighteen has exactly *nothing* to do with what was meaningful to me at age thirty-eight when I got my first and only tattoo.

So, I'm not telling you to wait twenty years on the tats. Just suggesting you let your adult personality gel first so you can find out what body art will continue to reflect your identity over the long haul. Yes, you can get tattoos lasered off at great expense, but is that really the right attitude to have going into this process? So, I've got to side with your mom, though perhaps for different reasons.

Where body art is concerned, think ahead and leave your teenage rebellion behind.

Piercing, on the other hand, has the distinct advantage of lasting just as long as you want it to. If you quit putting in the stud, you're going to lose all but a small scar. So, this is a fairly harmless area of experimentation as a teen. Just be sure to work with a professional. They're required to maintain a high quality of cleanliness that your best friend is not. So don't grab a needle and start stabbing. We have a different name for that. It's called self-mutilation.

The one exception is ear gauging. Before you email me about how old fashioned I am for saying this, hear me out. Gauging leaves a more permanent mark that, depending on the size of the gauge, can require plastic surgery to close. It's also far more obvious than many tattoos, which can be hidden or displayed, depending on clothing. If a perspective employer doesn't like your style, you can't simply take out your cool jewelry, as you would a nose ring, and put in a spacer.

In fact, if I were forced to choose between a tattoo and ear gauging, I'd go with the tat and put it somewhere that will only show when you want it to.

Bottom line: Where body art is concerned, think ahead and leave your teenage rebellion behind.

Julia Davidson: I have nothing against tattoos or body piercings. Many people I know have them. I just think that nowadays both get grouped in with the flashy extremes seen on TV and associated with a strange crowds of people, which is certainly not the case. If well thought out, tattoos can be meaningful and beautiful, just as piercings can be a good venue for self-expression, as long as the piercing is appropriate.

Personally, I think "under eighteen" tattoos and body piercings are okay in moderation and with proper safety precautions. The best body art I've seen is modest, tasteful, and serves its intended purpose as art. But when making a decision about body art, consider who you wouldn't want to see your tattoo or piercing—maybe your boss, principal, or grandparents—and then how often you will have to see those folks and what you'll be wearing when you do. Also remember that body art shouldn't be meant to offend.

Chances are these concerns and responsibilities ran through your mom's head when the words "tattoo" and "body piercing" first popped out of your mouth. Also, protesting that many people your age have body art may actually hurt your case. Teens can be irrational and when making a decision about a permanent hole or picture on your skin and then selling that idea to your parents, maturity is a must.

Lately, I've seen more belly button and ear cartilage piercings that are both well cared for and tasteful among my peers. If you're going for something more extreme like a tattoo or tongue or eyebrow piercing, ask for it as an eighteenth birthday present. Waiting shows respect for your mom's concern and gives you time to think all this through, both of which may put your mom at ease.

Spring Break

Dear Dr. Wes and Kelly,

My friends and I are planning a senior trip over spring break. By then, some of us will be eighteen and others still seventeen. Some of the parents are against it and some are okay with it. We want to convince them that all our friends should be able to go. This is our last year together and several of us are going out of state next fall. What tips can you give us?

Dr. Wes: I assume you mean tips for getting the 'rents on board and not for my personal travel preferences, although I do like the Florida Keys quite a bit. I'm glad you're asking months in advance. Too often, teens wait until February and are then upset when frustrated parents feel pressured to make a decision. That never wins you any points with the folks.

You're going to hit several snags on this. Just as you note, parents are not uniform in their views about whether senior trips are acceptable.

So, while one friend's parents may give thumbs-up, another's will say, "no way." Do *not* try and pit the proponent parents against the opponents or attempt to make anyone feel guilty for being stricter. This actually reduces the chances that the opponents will give in and increases their resentment if they do.

Another problem is age differences. Parents of seventeen-year-olds have a lot more to be concerned about than those with kids past the age of majority. Technically, parents can't really forbid an eighteen-year-old from doing something like this, but they can sure make it difficult. Underage kids not only need to have parental permission, but reasonable supervision to be certain they don't get caught up in some nightmarish child protective action. Your seventeen-year-old friends could easily be taken into custody by the police for no reason other than being underage and out-of-state with no parental supervision. Yes, I know that many teens have done this and everything came out just fine, but I've also been involved in other situations where all hell broke loose and things turned out very badly. So, give this some thought before expecting seventeen-year-olds to sign-on or asking their parents to sign-off.

This column is called Double Take, so this week Kelly and I differ in our optimism about the average senior's ability to manage such trips on their own. So, if you want to get the parents to go along, I suggest you invite them to go along—literally. That may sound like a huge, screeching bummer, but all I'm proposing is that a group of adults basically just hang out at the hotel while the seniors go about their business. That way they can afford their kids only the same amount of supervision they'd receive back home, except everyone moves the party south. Families report that this strategy has worked very well. I also strongly recommend that seniors *avoid* the standard spring break hotspots like Panama City and Fort Lauderdale. Even with parental oversight, these places are unwise for newly minted adults to hang out. Yes, I know that everything that happens in Padre happens in your hometown too, but it's a lot more intense, concentrated, and mind-blowing over Spring Break.

Finally, remember to consider costs. With a shaky economy, don't expect parents to pay the tab on your adventure, though they might wisely use the purse strings as an incentive to keep things within their comfort zone.

Kelly Kelin: Ah, Spring Break. While some kids are out with the family visiting relatives, others are taking their next body shot off a complete stranger. For parents, that kind of Spring Break is a nightmare. For kids, it's a declaration of independence.

Year after year, thousands of oversexed young adults flee to the popular beach spots, where tourism skyrockets and so does the underage drinking. It's only natural for parents to have reservations about unsupervised senior trips. Yet, I'm going to side with the teenagers on this one. Too often, I see parents preventing their children from amazing opportunities. What truly defines us as being "adults?" Is it when we turn eighteen? Or is it when the child was raised in a trusting environment where parents have instilled good morals and values? Let's face it: parents don't want their children to grow up. They try to hold on to every chance to keep them closer to home. It's not until they go off to college, notorious for its wild parties, that the ties to parents are shattered. Who is more likely to get drunk at this party, the girl who has been sheltered her whole life, or a child who was raised with and learned how to be mature around alcohol?

I know that this is your last chance to be together and your Spring Break will probably create some unforgettable memories, but it's unlikely all your friends will be able to attend. For those who do go, this is the ultimate chance to show your responsibility. Make sure you give your parents all the information and numbers of who is going and where you will be staying, and expect to pay for the trip yourself. By doing so, you will show that you are capable of being independent.

Kids must constantly prove themselves responsible. But how can we do that of we aren't given the opportunity? How is it possible for us to learn from our mistakes if our parents won't let us take the chance?

Juvenile Detention

Dear Dr. Wes and Marissa,

Is it okay for parents to put their out of control, anger-filled children in a juvenile detention center to get them help? And if not, what are other possibilities?

Marissa Ballard: I feel less qualified to answer this question than most because, fortunately for me, I have limited experience with juvenile detention. After some research, I found that, for most cases, one has to commit a crime or be a danger to society before being sent to JDC, and I'm not clear about whether either of those is true in your case.

If when using the term, "anger-filled" you mean he often has the teenage equivalent of a temper tantrum, then I don't think that is grounds for being locked up. However, if that temper has resulted in many fights and physical confrontations, then the child might require and even benefit from it.

A bad temper is something that can damage a person in more ways than one. Personal relationships will suffer if you can't effectively communicate without blowing your top, and no employer wants an employee who loses their cool at the drop of a hat.

If other options are not available to contain the teen in question, then JDC may be a choice, but families and society should really try to explore other solutions. I know we suggest therapy as the solution to everything, but, in this case, there could be a psychological or emotional problem or something else that has caused this anger.

> *Detention is not really there to "help" people. It's there to isolate, control, and maybe rehabilitate youth for antisocial behavior through punishment.*

Dr. Wes: Marissa is right. I've worked with a lot of these cases and actually wrote the book *Treating Families and Children in the Child Protective System*. I can tell you first hand that parents need to do everything possible to avoid using JDC in the way you describe. Detention is not really there to "help" people, like a social service agency. It's there to isolate, control, and *maybe* rehabilitate youth for antisocial behavior through punishment. That's an important function, but it's not a service for families with difficult kids. It's kid jail.

Such cases often involve some kind of psychological problem that detention centers and foster care are not designed to fix. Additionally, once either of these systems gets involved, kids and families are astonished at how quickly they lose control and things start happening that they don't necessarily like. Many parents have crossed my doorstep who sought out foster care or detention, only to regret it later.

Usually, therapy is a better alternative, but when things get way out of control, it takes more than a couple of sessions and a little good advice. It takes frequent, intensive, family-based therapy and often medication management. Individual therapy is not very helpful in these cases, even though it is often recommended.

I can understand how families facing turmoil, anger and violence feel there isn't anywhere else to turn. However, for difficult cases, there are community-based programs (available on an outpatient basis) that provide additional and more intensive services than once- or twice-a-week therapy. These programs may even be funded through what's called the "Medicaid Waiver," although many are presently facing budget cuts.

Try them, and any other reasonable alternative, before trying JDC.

11 LIVING IN THE REAL WORLD

Teenpolitik

Dear Dr. Wes and Ben,

I am a high school senior and part of a youth advocacy group that promotes youth and student influence in government and community decisions. We support education reform, dropout prevention, volunteer service, and post-schooling integration into the community. We currently have corporate funding as well as sponsorship from local, county, and state government officials. Our organization seeks to fight the apathy among teenagers by giving them a reason to care for their futures and their communities. As a new organization, our growth has been slow. Could you give us a plug to help us gain some sort of recognition from the community? Interested youth can find us on Facebook.

Dr. Wes: We're careful not to endorse any organization, but I certainly support your effort at political action and your stated goals. Double Take encourages teens to get involved in politics, since the future world belongs to you, not us aging baby-boomers. Now would be a great time for young people to get serious about policy issues, especially with so many looming problems before us.

The only defense against ignorance is information and teens would do well to: (a) find reliable sources about important political issues like college financial aid, job creation for young adults, access to health care, and a host of other concerns that may impact your short- and long-term futures; and (b) learn how to sensibly consume and interpret that data.

Never has so much information been instantly available, yet a great deal of it is meaningless crap. I hope your organization adds a goal of promoting critical data consumption and thinking skills among your teen constituents, so that they can make informed choices about what they believe and how they take sides. I realize schools have tried to take the lead on this, but a grassroots youth movement would really enhance that effort.

I don't fear an apathetic youth so much as I fear a youth that is passionate about something they know nothing about or only one side of.

So, good luck on your project. I'm thrilled to see young people standing up against apathy, which is far too prevalent among all age groups in our society.

Ben Markley: I came out of homeschooling and into public education. I was raised in a conservative household in a liberal town. You can imagine the culture shock. At school, I was told that George Bush was an oil-guzzling, war-mongering moron. At home, John Kerry was equally unpopular. As I've grown up, I've seen good friends both demonize and idolize parties and politicians. For what purpose? I don't know. I suspect many of them don't know either.

As a teenager, that is my great concern with politics. I don't fear an apathetic youth so much as I fear a youth that is passionate about something they know nothing about or only one side of.

Like Wes, I encourage you to go through the decision-making process, to be informed, to discern, and to conclude. If I could wish any one thing for this generation, it would be a discontentment with shortcut politics.

Volunteering

Dr. Wes: Volunteerism. The act of giving away a valued service with no expectation of personal gain. Many teens find ways to serve the community, often in search of a line item on a college application. That's terrific, but for others, including most of the Double Take writers over the years, volunteerism has taken on a greater significance in their lives. Ben is just back from a remarkable trip, working in a Romanian orphanage, not just for free but at a substantial cost, which he's now seeking to underwrite.

The lessons of volunteerism are priceless for teens and young adults, and the rest of us as well. To give away something of value is to give back to a local or global community that has given each of us a great deal more than we have earned. Too often, our idols are TV stars or other entertainers, some of whom contribute little more than their talent to the world. If they do chip in, it comes at no real sacrifice, just a nice tax deduction on a ginormous income. Real heroes are beneficent—they give away time, money, or effort to causes that truly help others.

I admire Ben's beneficence—as I do any teen who takes the volunteer road less traveled—not only for what he is doing for others but for what he's doing for himself. By landing squarely in the middle of a challenging and difficult situation, he's expanding not only his awareness of an entirely different world, but his empathy for those who live there. Having spent my early career working in public mental health and foster care, I know how difficult that can be and I applaud him for taking the plunge.

I encourage other teens and parents to join these sorts of efforts, even if you can't pull off a trip to Haiti or Romania. There are plenty of folks next door in need right now, and the rewards of service are just as great.

Ben Markley: Upon my return from Romania, I was asked to write a column on youth volunteerism based on my experience. Yet, I find I have nothing to say, beyond boring clichés about youth service. So, I won't.

Instead, I'll write about what really blew me away during my time in Romania—the generosity of the staff and kids at the orphanage. While my team did spend many hours cleaning out and organizing storehouses for the staff, I often felt as though I was the one being served. The staff constantly inquired about our needs and comfort, and the kids welcomed us from day one. They provided for our comfort, almost to a fault. This wasn't a project for them; this was their home, their everyday life.

The contrast is painful. I have to raise $2,000 and fly halfway around the world to inspire a sense of service in myself. My Romanian friends find that opportunity each day. Volunteering is great, but doing good for others shouldn't start with searching for an organization. It should begin at home, at school, at work, anywhere and everywhere you can lend a hand. It won't really fatten your résumé. It won't give you a great Facebook album.

It's just good.

Anti-Role Models

Dear Dr. Wes and John,

This isn't anything new, but lately there have been a lot of stories in the news about authority figures acting very badly. A cop got convicted of looking up a teenage girl's skirt. Some other officers didn't do anything to help a pregnant woman while they were arresting her and she miscarried. Teachers, coaches, and administrators have been in serious legal trouble. Now, my kids are in middle and high school and are basically saying there's no point in respecting the police or school personnel, and they think politics is a total joke. My kids are smart and aware, but it seems like they are getting cynical and I really don't know what to do. I want them to trust the basic goodness of people, but when I try and tell them that, I feel kind of gullible and stupid.

Dr. Wes: Unfortunately, cynicism *is* about as old as humanity itself. Yet, I've also found myself struggling more with this lately, as I see authority figures falling all over themselves to make bad decisions. I'm old enough to remember The Pentagon Papers, J. Edgar Hoover, Watergate, and the Kent State shootings. Now, post-9/11 we see violent extremists on one hand, and government officials all-too-ready to take away civil liberties on the other. Just what the terrorists ordered.

A wise person sees people as individuals, not as stereotypes.

In confronting this, I like to remind teens of the sense of duty New York police and fire fighters displayed as they entered the twin towers on 9/11, and the stories of heroism among our soldiers in the field. We each know fine teachers who spend their lives as highly educated persons in poorly paying jobs, because they believe in what they do. Each of these folks go against the grain of self-interest each day, to serve a higher social purpose. I encourage teens to seek in themselves this same sense of mission, so when they're standing face-to-face with difficulty, they will show similar courage and conviction.

But even as I read it back, I know that nice speech doesn't give the whole story, and to ignore that fact is a disservice to our teens. Instead,

I suggest a radically balanced view of human good and evil. Don't lump people or situations into the "evil" bin and others into the "good" bin. Instead, learn how and when to trust others, how to consume human interaction, and how to judge the character of people based on their behavior—not their job, or color, or age, or perceived level of authority.

It's a lot easier to say that all policemen are "Officer Friendly" and all sex offenders are "sick strangers," but the truth is that each person has a capacity to help and harm; to love and hate; to humanize and dehumanize. Each of us chooses which way we're going to go every day of our lives, and much of that choosing begins in adolescence. That's the nature of free will.

A wise person sees people as individuals, not as stereotypes. She does not generalize the bad behavior of a few officers to the police force; or the stellar conduct of one teacher to the entire faculty. I'll admit that this is a much less comforting idea than simple naïveté or cynicism, but I promise that it's a lot more helpful.

John Murray: Whether it's teachers, police, soldiers, or priests, the media is always looking for dirt on the people we trust. We repay the media by watching their programs and upping their ad revenue. But we mustn't judge a whole class of people based on the mistakes of a few and even avoid judging those we know are guilty. Many of the "Hester Prynns" in our society face mitigating circumstances, such as family history, that we never hear about. Instead of seeking out the faults in others, we should focus on becoming the role models we wish to see.

Sometimes, I imagine what would happen if Hollywood made a film about my worst moments. If the public were to discover all three of my sins, I'm not sure I could stand the humiliation. But why do we expect angelic coverage of our role models, people whose lives are on camera 24/7? You never hear about the businesses that could have stolen money but chose not to. In the media, one slipup is enough to condemn a person, even a group of people, and a thousand good works will not redeem them.

As for the dismal state of politics, Americans have no one to blame but themselves. Surely our Senate Majority Leader makes more important decisions than Paris Hilton. Yet, only fifteen percent of us know his name. When you ignore your elected officials, you release them from accountability. When you don't read up on the current events, you open yourself to manipulation. Each of us is now $30,000 in debt due to a bipartisan failure to control the national budget. Congress gets away with it because they know we don't pay any attention. If Americans don't like this, they need to turn their cynicism into action.

It's hard enough to obey an order you know is correct. It's even tougher to obey one you hate. But we must respect our authorities, even when they make bad choices. Bashing police will not make better officers. Instead, we must recognize the imperfections inherent in all human beings, and save judgment for the jury.

Building Your Social Network

John Murray: The world is a huge place, and it would be foolhardy to try and tackle it alone. Whether you're looking for homework help or trying to find a job, knowing more people will help to get you ahead. Social networking is the process of gathering a large pool of people from which you can draw support. Businesses often devote huge sums of money to this task. Up-and-coming teens should get a head start by meeting people right away. Here are my tips for building your network.

Always keep an outgoing attitude. Whenever you attend parties, weddings, or funerals, make a beeline for people you don't know. Most will appreciate the company. Ask them questions about themselves (people love that subject), and make every effort to remember their names. You may be surprised at the ways these people can pop up again in your life.

Keep in touch with connections you already have. It sounds like a cliché, but sending cards is always a good idea. Try to collect cheap cards, often available in 99-cent packs. At the beginning of each month, fill out a card for everyone who has a birthday that month. It may seem time consuming to write all those cards in one sitting, but it makes quite an impression on the recipient. Also, remember to write down the names of everyone who sends you cards or money for the holidays, and send thank-you notes promptly.

No discussion of social networking would be complete without mentioning Facebook, which provides an incredible opportunity to be "in the know" about your community. With the click of the mouse you can learn about upcoming events, read up on your friends' lives, or create an online résumé. Just remember, a wall post will never substitute for face-to-face conversation, and of course there are plenty of people who simply aren't inclined to use these sites.

Dr. Wes: Social networking comes easily for some. For others, it's like a painful day at the dentist. But love it or hate it, there's no arguing with John on the importance of this topic. When discussing a job search, you've heard cynics say, "It's not what you know, but who you know." They're rarely wrong. Ask anyone and you'll find very few self-made men or women. Most have used social contacts at least as effectively as their knowledge or skill.

Billionaire and New York Mayor Mike Bloomberg started out as the son of poor immigrants. On his way up the ladder, he once worked for a fellow who loved to smoke at the start of each business day. Bloomberg made sure he just happened to be there too, with cigarettes to offer the guy every morning. Ingratiating? Maybe. Good for that guy's health? Definitely not. But Bloomberg might finance his own run for the presidency now, and that's saying something about the value of making friends and influencing people. By the way, that's also the name of Dale Carnegie's famous book on this topic. With its first printing in 1937, it was still at number ninety-nine last week on Amazon.com with nearly 400 four-star reviews. So, this topic is far from new and still absolutely relevant.

The real value of online social networking is not just in forming relationships that only exist out there, but in creating and enhancing real world connections.

So, where does this leave the shy people? In the market for social skills enhancement. More than anyone else, the shy and awkward need human involvements, even as they struggle to find and manage them. The Internet has been a blessing for many people in building relationships. Yet, even with aggressive use of online social networking or (for the over-eighteen crowd) online dating sites, you still have to do the face-to-face work at some point. So, the real value of online social networking is not just in forming relationships that only exist out there, but in creating and enhancing real world connections.

Most of the socially awkward teens I see are really amazing when you get past their fearfulness. Working with an adult mentor or even a skilled peer can help connect the dots so you can grow your social network in the ways John describes.

For those who are struggling a bit more, therapy, social coaching, and matching younger teens in church, school, or other natural settings can also help. Regardless of which path you choose in life, social networking is a tool that none of us can toss just because it's hard or uncomfortable at times.

Sucky and Awesome

Dear Dr. Wes and Julia,

Why is life so sucky? And why is it so awesome?

Dr. Wes: This pithy little note is one of the best pieces of teen verse I've heard in a while. All at once, you've summed up the core duality of life. While adults also struggle with this yin-yang, the two ends of that spectrum are never more intense than when you're about fifteen. So, whether you realized it or not, you hit on a serious piece of philosophical tradition that touches on the ever-present balance between things that are good with those that are not.

This "problem of evil" has been studied for generations, and asks the question of how so many bad things can exist in the presence of a loving and all-powerful God. Since this is a column based on psychology, I'll leave it to you to seek out the philosophical or theological answers, but your thoughtful mind should at least know that your question is important.

No matter how sucky life has been so far, we still have choices that can move it in the direction of becoming awesome.

Rather than dwell on "why," however, I suggest you turn your inquiry over to the question of "how." As in, how are you going to act on your world to make it less sucky and more awesome? Yes, we're all products of our life experience, family, school, socioeconomic background, etc. None of us can go back and choose different lives, filled with more money or less dysfunction. We can't force our peer group to act with greater empathy or our politicians to shut up about ridiculous non-issues and get serious about the real and frightening ones all around us. The children of high conflict divorces may try desperately, but in the end it's tough to force parents to get along.

Yet, in the end, we have to believe in free will and our ability to rise above the sucky nature of whatever hand we've been dealt rather than contribute to the overall level of personal or global suckiness. I know this is hard to believe when you're a teenager, when you feel you have no power over anything. But there is always something you can do to make a small change that may grow into a larger one if you nurture it enough.

No matter how sucky life has been so far, we still have choices that can move it in the direction of becoming awesome. The abused child does not have to grow up to be an abuser. The child of a person who committed suicide does not have to follow his parent's path. The young person who was molested can work hard to avoid sexually abusive partners in adulthood. The teen who made mistakes, even terrible ones, can make amends and grow up to be a fine and caring adult.

Unfortunately, that question of "why" is where kids, and quite a few adults, get stuck. They get down about the many sadnesses of life, become disillusioned, and begin to turn against themselves. One of the really awesome things about life in our part of the world is that help is available for young people who want it. If your life sucks, find an adult professional—a teacher, therapist, social worker—who is well-trained to believe in free will and who can help you discover yours.

Suckiness will be with us always, but if you seek the right path, it tends to be drowned out by a much larger deposit of awesomeness.

Good luck on your journey.

Julia Davidson: I, too would love to launch into a philosophical study about the essence of "sucky" and the history of "awesome" and how the two coexist, but I know no single, direct answer to the question. It depends on your religion, your outlook on life, what goes down as "sucky" or "awesome" in your book, and other subjective factors.

My personal "awesomes" include cappuccino foam, good jokes, blankets, and soap. Personal "suckys" consist of red peppers, rude clerks, tardiness, and being ignored. Each day these things register different levels of reaction in me, the "awesomes" and "suckys" cancelling, adding, compounding, until my day either has more "awesomes" (a good day) or more "suckys" (a bad day), or nothing at all. My tally can be pretty sporadic. I can look back and say, "Man, I had an awesome week. But Wednesday, jeez." Of course, the more you find your day was "bad," the more evidence you'll find to prove it, the more you'll believe it and pretty soon, BAM! A reasonable day can turn into a rather sucky one.

Spontaneity and impulse are the hallmarks of our generation, forcing people to be more extreme and forceful with their emotions. When asked about your day, most people expect a short "good" or "bad"— simple polar opposites. There's rarely room for the explanation of how this was "a chill day," "a practical day" or a "mysterious" one. The asker has already moved on to the next person. Really, life is what you make it and limiting it to either "sucky" or "awesome" closes off so many other new possibilities.

So, have your "suckys" and your "awesomes" as I do, but don't forget to consider the "different," the "marvelous" and even the "off-limits" to remember that life is not simply sucky or awesome, but a million other things as well.

12 INTO THE FUTURE

The Best Years of Our Lives?

Dear Dr. Wes and John,

My mom says these are the best years of my life; that I should make use of them. I am fifteen, and if these are the best years of my life, I do not want to be around for the rest.

Dr. Wes: This was a poignant little note and I appreciate your raising the issue. It's kind of a tradition for parents to try and lift the spirits of their teens by recalling the many virtues of their own adolescence. Think of it as the reverse of "When I was a kid, I had to walk to school…in blizzards uphill…there *and* back." In this rosy, "best years of your life" memoir, parents want you to be thankful for your youth and not miss all the great things it offers you.

Never judge the prospects for your future life by your years as an adolescent. The two have nothing to do with each other.

You see, the longer adults are away from their own teen years, the more they think those times must have been really terrific. We didn't have a mortgage or credit card bills to pay. We didn't have to get up every day and work forty or fifty hours a week. Love was fresh and agonizingly intense. We had our friends close at hand and the times we shared made memories for a lifetime. We could desperately yearn for freedom, pulling wildly against the forces of authority, without really suffering adult consequences. Best of all, everything was new and open for exploration. So, when your mom looks back, she just can't help but cheer you on.

I think, however, that she's forgetting all the yucky crap we had to go through as teens. For many, these years are filled with rejection, embarrassment, and perpetual awkwardness. As you leave grade school, some of those great friends turn out to be less than trustworthy and many do not last until high school graduation.

The kids I see, even the excellent students, constantly remind me of how stressful school has become. With love comes inevitable pain and sometimes problematic dating patterns that hang around much too long. Teen demands for freedom cause conflict, which can leave hard feelings at home. New and novel things are untested, often posing a potential for unexpected harm. So, I understand the frustration you feel when Mom encourages you to sit back and let the joys of adolescence wash over you like warm rainwater. She seems a little disconnected from your daily reality, doesn't she?

I would instead urge you to *never* judge the prospects for your future life by your years as an adolescent. As a psychologist and recovering teenage boy, I can tell you that the two have nothing to do with each other. Who you are at twenty-five, thirty-five, and beyond will depend less on who you are at fifteen than how you organize your life between now and then. Enjoy the good things that adolescence has to offer— there really are many—and see if you can sidestep some of the screwed up ones.

To give up now is like buying a ticket and a bucket of popcorn at the movie theater, watching previews of other movies, and then leaving just as the opening credits start. The really good stuff is yet to come, and as you become more able to choose what to do with your life, who to do it with, and when to do it, you'll also discover yourself and the things that make life truly meaningful.

If stuff is getting too depressing or you really are having thoughts of ending it all, please visit with a therapist at once so she can work with you to find the future you deserve.

John Murray: "These are the times that try men's souls." These words, spoken by Thomas Paine, were initially meant to describe the late 1700's, but could be applied again and again throughout history. Thomas Paine and your mom can accurately point to privileges that are no longer available, as well as hardships that plague modern life. But to mull over the joys or trials of previous eras is not only delusional, listening to it can be a real "Paine" to those at an earlier stage of life.

Many people wish they lived in another decade, mistakenly believing that "life was simpler back then." Perhaps you'd like to live in the 1940's when gas was cheap and chivalry a way of life. Or maybe you yearn for the 1960's, when the world was fresh and "the revolution" was imminent. Yet, historians note that, while every era had its disappointments, the number of people who reported feeling happy never varied much. Perhaps this is because satisfaction depends not on being dealt the best cards in the deck, but in finding the aces already in your hand.

Yes, the teen years can be harsh. Even if you do survive the loneliness, anger, peer pressure, incompetent teachers, and endless standardized testing, you still have to worry about body image, paying for college, maintaining grades, betrayal, and ultra-competitive extracurricular activities.

Take comfort in the fact that you made it through middle school and you'll make it through high school, too. In fact, I found high school a far more comfortable experience than my junior high days. As long as you stick to the basics (turning in assignments, balancing school and friends, staying away from drugs, etc.), you'll do fine.

The best years of your life will always be the next ones, and always be dependent upon what you make of them.

College Bound...Or Not

John Murray: With college application season kicking into full speed, Wes and I are dedicating this column to choosing colleges. If you're a senior, colleges may be pressuring you to apply on early-decision. This allows them to make a quick admission verdict in exchange for a promise not to apply anywhere else if you're admitted. I think this discriminates against low-income students who need to compare financial aid offers in the spring, but even if you're applying for regular admission, try to begin the process as soon as possible to allow for any last-minute crises.

While the average wage of a college graduate is nearly double that of non-grads, *where* you go to college will have far less of an impact than how you perform in school. A study comparing 1976 Ivy League

Graduates to those who were accepted to an Ivy League school, but then chose to attend a less prestigious college, found that the Ivy League Grads had *the same median income* twenty years after graduation. Half the members of the U.S. Senate attended public colleges.

There's no "wrong" college to attend, and what is important for one student may be insignificant for another. While I'll weigh ROTC programs heavily in choosing my college, others might place more emphasis on sports, social atmosphere, or the reputation of a particular academic department.

Cost is obviously a front-burner issue for many parents, but if you're interested in an expensive school, apply anyway. In the spring, you will learn about your financial aid eligibility, and then you can compare price tags. Also consider location and size. While some students may yearn for the independence of a university far from home, others prefer being able to swing by the old house and see the parents on short notice.

Whether you hit the books again three months after high school graduation, or wait a year or two, keep further learning in your plan.

Once you decide what is important to you in selecting a college, investigate schools with a variety of sizes, cultures, locations and admission standards, and try to imagine how you would feel attending each one. Meanwhile, invest time and energy in visiting nearby colleges—even those you are not interested in—to get a sense of their culture. Finally, choose four to six schools you would most like to attend and GET THOSE APPLICATIONS ROLLING!

Dr. Wes: If you're headed to college this fall, then I'm with John all the way. However, I'd like to back up and address a more fundamental issue—whether to go to college or not. While there's probably some form of post-high school education for everyone, college may not be it. One of the most common and unfortunate situations I see are young people who did not really think through the choice to go to college and/or parents who pressured them to go anyhow. Sometimes this works out fine. Often it does not.

It might seem that if given a choice, most late teens would rather go to school than toil away at the various food service, construction, manufacturing, or retail jobs available to you. However, that point is often realized only after you've actually worked those jobs. There's something to be said for laying out a year if you really don't believe you're ready to take the big plunge that John so accurately describes. Just don't spend that year underemployed, living off the folks, partying hard, and sleeping in. In fact, I recommend that parents be pretty strict with non-college-bound grads. If instead, you spend a year or two out of high school, working, putting back a little money, having some fun, and growing up, you're miles ahead of any reluctant, unhappy freshman who's counting the days until bombing out.

On the other hand, I see a number of "nontraditional" or "returning" students who wish they had *not* taken this road and stayed in school. College can be a lot tougher later on, when you have a family, full time work, and/or financial concerns.

So, before blowing off school completely, the other thing to consider is whether trade school, junior college, military service, or vocational technical school is more your speed. I've seen many young people go into cosmetology or auto repair, and then use their increased earning power to finance further study. If your family is disappointed in this decision, hand them this column and encourage them to reconsider. Nearly any vocational training is useful, and the starting wage for an auto mechanic is pretty decent. The same is true for computer systems, networking, and information technology jobs.

As John points out, a high school diploma, besides allowing you to enter the next level of education, offers little edge down the road of life. Whether you hit the books again three months after high school graduation, or wait a year or two, I encourage you to keep further learning in your plan. It's one of the best investments of time and money you'll make.

College Advice From the Experts

Dr. Wes: This week we're privileged to have the last four Double Take co-authors back for some solid advice on making a successful transition to college. So, I'll get out of the way and leave the rest of the column to the real experts.

Marissa Ballard, Pittsburg State: In the fall, an eager group of young adults will embark on their freshman year of college. If they are anything like me, they're in for an awakening—rude or otherwise. Each experience is unique. However, I'll offer these simple words of advice:

Dorms Are Ugly. I'll admit I cried when I first saw my room. The linoleum was peeling, the ceiling sagged. An area rug and some creative poster placement can do wonders, so come prepared.

Wash Your Sheets...Often. Your bed is not your own when you live with fifty college students. I've returned to find a cigarette butt between my sheets, wondering how it got there. Trust me, you're better off safe than sorry.

Live With Strangers. What could be more fun than living with your besties, right? Wrong. I too was skeptical of this advice. Junior year, I got an apartment with a friend. Within three months, we went from sharing clothes to her ransacking our living room and moving out.

College presents more freedom and independence to decide what truly freaks you out, turns you on, and makes you happy.

Graduate. This is not a guideline. It's a requirement. Don't join the ranks of those who give up after their first year. Commit yourself to finish what you started. You won't regret it.

John Murray, Texas A&M: My advice is to create. Ruthlessly, recklessly, and without permission. Most people are nice, but when it comes down to it, most of our actions are motivated by self-interest. We seek friends who can provide fun experiences, jobs that offer decent money, and courses that yield a degree. We look for ways to cut corners, to provide other people with the minimum we can get away with. Yet, the most direct route to prosperity is creating value for others. Like elephants surrounding the waterhole, people gravitate towards those who can provide value. A person who creates value will always be in demand, which will grant them access to the lion's share of resources.

So, what does this have to do with college? College is the perfect opportunity to learn how to create. Don't slip into the trap of waiting for others to create for you. Instead of watching Jersey Shore reruns, host a Jersey Shore theme party. Instead of reading Cliffnotes, write your own detailed notes and give them out to your classmates. Not only will you improve your own creative skills, but your popularity, too.

Julia Davidson, freshman Macalester College: Revel like an elephant in a mud puddle. College presents more freedom and independence to decide what truly freaks you out, turns you on, and makes you happy. If you let your interests and whims guide you, you won't have to fake enjoying yourself.

Don't forget the basics of self-care. Vitamins. Sleep. Good food. Exercise. Yes, Mr. Pibb and pizza and tacos taste awesome for breakfast, but your body will start retaliating. The freshman poundage, feeling like crap, and getting sick are direct results of how you take care of yourself. Be gentle.

You pay a lot to go to college. Make sure it's worth it. Are you happy? Do you enjoy what you are learning? Do you feel like you're growing in your experiences and education? If not, you are wasting your time and money.

Don't expect to get it all at once. We don't hold six-year-olds to their proclamations to become cowboys, so we shouldn't expect every freshman who says they're going to med school to actually do it. Don't count this normal flux against anyone or yourself. College is for change and uncertainty.

Finally, find what works for you and stick to it.

And in case none of that works for you, everyone knows how to make Ramen noodles and do their laundry, right?

Kelly (Kelin) Woods, University of Kansas: The transition from high school to college may seem romantic to those ready to embark on their own adventures in life. Yet, it doesn't take long for students to realize that there are important, adult decisions to make. Living on your own can impose many obstacles. How you handle these choices is the big factor in your life success. For those of you about to start your own adventures, here is my advice.

Attend class. Most of my teachers don't take attendance in their lectures, making it tempting to skip. Trust me, it's much easier to get a good grade when you attend class.

Learn to budget. Despite Julia's encouragement, living off of Ramen noodles gets old after a while. Open a savings account. Every time money heads your direction deposit some. This will help you learn to remain independent and financially stable. You'll be surprised how quickly you begin to save money. Also, start cutting coupons. There are deals all around, yet few really use them.

Don't get too caught up in the college party. Life isn't measured by the number of beer pong games you win. It's measured through experience and willingness to master yourself. Remember, this is your bridge to becoming an adult. Now is the time to act like one.

I'm Not Ready

Dear Dr. Wes and Ben,

I'm going to college this fall and I'm just now realizing I don't know if I can live on my own. My mom or dad have done everything for me all my life, and while I liked it at the time, now I'm kind of mad at them. I'm afraid I'm helpless and school is, like, two months away.

Ben Markley: The good news is that you're far from alone. A lot of us don't quite realize all the things our parents do for us until we have to buy our own groceries, pay own bills, sign ourselves up for things and do all the other tedious things we figured were always taken care of.

Here's more good news—you don't have to live completely on your own. There will be plenty of life-experienced people at college, and you'll want to find a few that can really help you through your first few months of feeling things out. Also, it never hurts to give your parents a call when you come up against something you know nothing about.

Independence is the opposite of freedom. It's about taking responsibility for yourself and accepting the consequences.

Living on your own doesn't mean knowing exactly what to do in every situation, but it does mean finding what you're capable of doing and when you need help. It means using your friends and family as counselors, not crutches. It means owning your decisions and not letting someone else make up your mind.

This stage of your life is scary, but it's exciting, too. Embrace it!

Dr. Wes: I can't improve on Ben's advice, so I'll just confirm that over my years of practice I have observed a growing trend among parents to over-function on behalf of their children. Teenagers need a bunch of things in life, and near the top of the list is natural consequence. Therapists Foster Cline and Jim Fay have made careers out of guiding parents to "parent with love and logic" and there's good sense in their approach. Instead, many parents often try to make their children's lives perfectly bearable by providing excesses in everything from possessions to freedom, trying to shield them from consequences.

The more teens can resist their parents' tendency to over-provide, the better off the teen will be when facing adulthood.

As teens, you beg, borrow, demand and steal your freedom, and that is just as it should be, because that's your job. But you're far less inclined to accept and manage the independence that comes with it. So, parents are better off tempering kids for life rather than helping them avoid it. Freedom seems so fun at seventeen. It offers the promise of living without someone standing over your shoulder questioning your next move and then setting limits on it. But in your letter you've shown considerable maturity in realizing something many of your peers don't until they're really out on their own—independence is the opposite of freedom. It's about taking responsibility for yourself on a daily basis and accepting the consequences for your actions, large and small.

Because you see this, you're actually in a better spot to handle adult life than you might imagine. I'm not saying it will be comfortable, particularly if your folks overdid it as you grew up. No doubt your first year of college will be a mixed up jumble that combines the glory of freedom and the agony of independence. I'm sure your parents will be there to back you up if you need them, but I'd challenge you to do your best to use their support less and less as you find your own two legs to stand on.

You'll get there.

Goodbye My Love

Dr. Wes: It's coming. I call it "Anti-Valentine's Day." That day in mid-August when graduated seniors leave high school loves behind and head off to the Big-U. Whether you're moving across town or across the country, maintaining a relationship with someone back in high school or at another University can be challenging. In fact, the "Turkey Drop" is a common euphemism for dumping your devoted sweetheart during Thanksgiving break of freshman year.

Not a very pretty picture, is it?

There are about three ways to handle this situation, and the secret to making each of them work is *clarity* and *communication*. Both partners have to be voluntarily on the same page, know what page that is, and actually choose a path rather than just default to what seems easy or comfortable.

Staying Together. This romantic option is made a bit more practical today by video chat and social networking, which allows couples to remain at least electronically close. With planning and lots of travel, this can work out okay for a few of the most dedicated couples, but it will fail for the rest. Even if distance isn't a factor, it takes a lot of self-denial and discipline to remain true to someone who isn't playing a part in your daily life, and it's impossible to learn how you'll really fare once you're offline and living real life together.

Dating on school breaks. This can get pretty dicey, especially for those who are staying local for college, but if you want to extend your high school romance, it's possible to break up for the school year and reconnect on holidays. It's just not easy. You have to really break up in the interim, which means *no questions* asked about what the partner has been doing during the school year. It also means that one cannot ethically maintain a serious relationship while at college without revealing their hometown dating situation, and vice versa.

Breaking Up. Sadly, saying goodbye is the most plausible scenario. Unfortunately, many couples say they're ending their relationships, and then stay in contact and up in each other's business, as if they were still together. That's as bad an idea as I can think of, and endlessly stretches out the painful breakup. Ben addresses a more humane way next.

Ben Markley: As a recent graduate, I've seen this issue, up close and personal, in the lives of my friends. There's no easy way to deal with it. It's hard to break up with someone, especially when neither of you really wants to. As Wes says, depending on your relationship, distance is not necessarily fatal. My sister and her high school sweet-heart overcame the graduation dilemma and are getting married!

For those going down the more common route, here's some advice on breaking up.

- **Consider the timing.** I would argue that sooner is better than later. You'll want some time at home, surrounded by family and friends, to work through things.
- **Talk it out.** If your relationship was serious, then you'll both need closure. Be gentle but reasonable.
- **Move on.** Of course it's going to be awkward, but you need to acclimate to being a single student. You don't need to sever all ties, but get some distance between you two.

This is a hard time, but it will only pass if you deal with it.

Dysfunctional Family, Dysfunctional Future?

Dear Dr. Wes and Ben,

I am twenty-years-old, but I hope you'll still answer my question. My family was really dysfunctional when I was a teenager and now that I'm on my own I am getting more worried that I will never get over this and have a normal life. What can I do to be free of what I grew up with?

Ben Markley: When you feel like you're at the bottom, an important first step is giving the top a reality check. As seniors, we think everybody else knows where they're going to college and what they're going to do when they get there; that everybody has everything already figured out. But that's a skewed perspective. Everybody isn't nearly as well put together as we think.

Similarly, the families to which you compare your own probably suffer from plenty of their own dysfunctions. Family is not an easy thing; ask any parent. There are tensions and conflicts within even the most loving, stable families. Coming from a tight family is certainly a great boost when you're sent out into the world, but I know a number of incredible people—people whom I admire—who come from rough families. There's always the potential to be beaten down by hard circumstances, but also the chance to grow stronger.

The fact that you're writing with this question says that you understand enough to get started on the journey toward a better tomorrow.

Biologically, we are confined to one family that we don't get to choose. Beyond biology, however, there's nothing that restricts us to one family. Technically, I have one brother, but I know a handful of guys with whom I share an incredible sense of brotherhood. Some are younger and look up to me while others are big "brothers" who help me when I'm at a loss. No one can replace my dad, but there are older men whom I consult in the same way a son would go to a father. Some found me. Others, I sought out myself.

The best way to find these people is to be honest with them, to put some faith in others and open up to them. Who knows? Maybe they need that sense of family just as much as you need them.

Dr. Wes: I'm with Ben. You can't choose the family you came from, but you can certainly choose the one you want to create, not only in your friendship circle, but in who you marry and how you raise your own kids.

Psychology has given us many valuable things over the last hundred or so years. The "dysfunctional family" is not among them. I'm not proposing that they don't exist, simply that from Sigmund Freud on, the problems we face growing up have been turned into a catch-all excuse for not getting up and doing what needs to be done. There's little doubt that if you're lucky enough to come from a home with strong parenting, you'll face fewer difficulties adjusting to adult life. If your family abused you, were alcoholics, or engaged you in a high conflict divorce, the process of growing up will be harder. But many young people have used those bad examples as a guide on exactly *what not to do,* and found a way to succeed. The fact that you're writing with this question says to me that you understand enough to get started on the journey toward a better tomorrow.

Another questionable psychological principle is encouraging people to express each and every feeling they have. Instead, while your feelings about your family are valid and important, they actually have nothing to do with living a normal and productive life. Experience your pain, and joy, and resentment, and hope, and then decide with your mind exactly who you are going to become. You are not a puppet, tied to the way your family taught you to be. From a genetic standpoint, you probably share some brain chemistry with them (anxiety, depression, ADHD, etc.), but you are free to address those problems head on, even if your family didn't.

I certainly don't want to seem insensitive to whatever you've been through, but as I've gotten older, I'm beginning to see many kids I served through the most dire of circumstances—foster care, disturbed divorces, the death of a parent—grow up and emerge as competent, loving, giving people. You can do it, too.

Find a mentor, some other worthy adult who is willing to give you time and guidance, and then follow his lead. Or you could pick a famous person you'd like to emulate, study her life, and see how she made it work. You may be shocked to see just how many people turned a bad childhood into a great life as an adult. The choices of the past are not up to you. Those you make in the future are.

Pomp and Circumstance

Dr. Wes: Congratulations, seniors! Now that you've had a week to recuperate, we'll share our advice to new grads for this summer and beyond.

Travel. Nothing is a more fitting graduation gift than travel, even if you give it to yourself.

While you may have chances to do this as a college student, the summer following senior year is a great time to get started. Whether you can finance an overseas trip or just pack up your sleeping bag, fill up the tank, and drive across America, there's a lot to see and explore with your newfound adulthood. I'll never forget when a good friend and I spent two weeks driving to and from Washington, DC right after walking the stage. Now, I go there all the time, but the trip seemed terribly exciting when I was eighteen.

> *Don't rush through the next four years as if they were just wrapping paper on the real presents of life. Savor the moments.*

You may have problems renting motel rooms because you're under twenty-one, so check ahead before you leave. It's also best to take a friend or two, but remember to keep your heads. Part of taking a senior road trip is getting into adventures. The other part is playing smart. Getting into trouble as a juvenile is one thing. Ending up in the Bojangles County Jail as a young adult is a more serious matter.

Avoid Credit. Among the worst burdens society thrusts off on our new graduates is the infamous credit card, car loan, and worst of all, payday loan. Even student loans can quickly become excessive and they only pay dividends if you graduate and work for a decent wage. For the most part, just say no to plastic cards. Any loan you take during your first years of adulthood should be designed for one thing: Getting ahead in life.

Avoid Cars. I know this is sacrilegious in America, but cars are huge money pits for young adults, especially at three or four bucks a gallon for gas. If a bike will do for the first year of college or work, give it a shot. If you have to buy a car, get one that combines low cost, high reliability, and fuel efficiency. I know this seems obvious, but that doesn't seem to impact anyone until several $75 trips through the gas station per month, and a couple of minor $750 car repair bills.

Try Something Different. You're going to be caught up in a certain routine for most of your life. You'll see many of the same people every day, work at the same job, go to the same places, and so on. That sounds horribly boring right now, but it's the way life is for most of us. While you're still young, try working in a different kind of job than what you'd expect to do down the road. Get to know some people that aren't like you.

Fight for Your Goals, But Move On When Things Aren't Working. This is another of those "balance" issues we're always talking about. One shouldn't give up on anything (school, relationships, jobs, etc.) without trying to work things out. We are an impatient society, and if anything goes wrong, we have a tendency to jump to the next big thing before we've finished the first. On the other hand, if you come to the realization that someone or something isn't good for you, put the relationship in your past.

You're going to wake up tomorrow and be halfway through life. Keeping bad baggage is just as bad as failing to stick to something good in life.

John Murray: Here's a list from a new graduate, for new graduates:

Plan, Plan, Plan. The most overwhelming part of transitioning to adulthood is the amount of responsibility immediately thrust upon you. With so much to do, it's easy to get caught up in emotions or impulse. That's why it's vital to make a plan for tackling college. At the beginning of the year, decide what grades you want and design a general game plan for studying. Create a budget to pay for your basic essentials, and maybe some recreation, without overspending. When you go to a party and *before* you take the first sip, decide how much you will drink and how you will get home. Setting limits may sound restrictive, but it actually frees you from mistakes and regrets.

Find Your Sweet Spot. One of my best teachers told me that as soon as you find the career you love, you never have to work again. As Wes said, you will probably find yourself pulling the same job year after year for the rest of your life, so it better be something you can tolerate. There are hundreds of courses available at college, so take a thorough look at what's available. If you, like sixty percent of college students, find your first major isn't what you expected, don't be afraid to change. Read up on a variety of subjects in order to get a taste of what's out there. With so many career options these days, you'd do well to understand your choices.

Cherish the Moment. This is good advice for anyone, but college students are especially gifted with unique opportunities. At no other time will you be surrounded by so many people, and faced with so many options and activities. Don't rush through the next four years as if they were just wrapping paper on the real presents of life. Savor the moments. And for now, don't worry about the future. As a character in South Park once said, "There's a time and a place for everything, and it's called college."

Through The Lens

Dr. Wes: Double Take came out of a discussion between Jenny Kane and I about the need for parents and teenagers to have a common forum to share ideas and advice. We thought this would be an opportunity to put that dialog in print. I'm always surprised when I Google the column to see it appear on webpages all around the world, some agreeing with us, some just posting, and some calling us strange things in foreign tongues that we fortunately do not understand. But we're being read, and for that we are grateful.

This week brings Jenny's last column. In appreciation for her work this year, I wanted to yield my space for whatever topic she thought most relevant to teenagers and their parents. I also want to wish her the best of times at Western Kentucky University this fall.

Jenny Kane: As a photographer, I have seen high school through the eye of a lens. I watched as some people rose to their best and others fell to their worst. I was there to capture the basketball team winning yet another game and to see class-mates grow and change. As a

I will be the same core person wherever I go. I will change and grow, but also take with me the experiences that made me who I am so far.

member of the yearbook staff, I saw it as my duty to remind others of their joy, although it will take most people many years to understand the significance of a book documenting their high school days. Even the yearbook could not adequately capture the joys, tears, the self-destructive behavior, and the mistakes each of us have made along the way. I hope that my photos and writings will help us remember good times and learn from the bad.

During high school, I lost some friendships because of the decisions others made about drugs, and I have lost other friendships because I was too selfish to let those people be happy. I lost a best friend, one I had throughout my hellish time in junior high, because I thought I knew what was best for her and I forced her to make a choice between that and our friendship. I know now that you shouldn't give others unfair ultimatums, and no matter how hard it may be at times, you have to let friends do what they feel is right. You can stay by their side and let them cry on your shoulder, but you have to let them learn.

I moved here in seventh grade. I thought it would be a fresh start, that I could just leave my grade school mistakes behind, not realizing that it isn't where you go, or how many miles you are away from where you used to live, it doesn't change you. Only you can do that. As I leave for college, I have learned I will be the same core person wherever I go. I will change and grow, but also take with me the experiences that made me who I am so far.

I will also know who my true friends are after I leave. They'll be the ones who take time out of their busy schedules to just drop in; to call me up on my birthday and sing me a tune, even though we both know that they can't sing. They are the ones who will have my back no matter what stupid thing I do. I've made it through adolescence because I was able to find those true friends.

My less fortunate relationships came because I wasn't able to be that kind of a friend to others; wasn't ready to just be myself and find others out there who will accept me. Too often, I put up with friends who were mean to one another and to me, and watched unkind words rip apart relationships. Like many girls my age, I tried to make people like me by being someone I was not. I made myself into this ditzy girl because I thought people couldn't or wouldn't accept the real me. They might make fun of the person I pretended to be, and I thought that was fine, because it wasn't really me. Yet, over time I *became* that ditz, and it took a girl in my American Lit class to remind me of my true identity.

Ever since, I've been trying to look that way at others, and I've found some pretty interesting people—specifically, a bunch of geeky gamers who hadn't been out in the light for what looked like a couple of years. But I learned a lot from them, and now I'm slowly but surely overcoming my assumptions about who people are supposed to be and, instead, accepting them for who they are.

Every teen has had that feeling of wanting to crawl up in a ball and disappear, and I found that the main thing that we wished for during those moments was someone to talk to and really be there for us. So, I urge you to reach out and be that true friend.

Sometimes that's all a person needs.

Finding The Aces

Dr. Wes: As John leaves the column, he is, like so many of his peers, embarking on an entirely new journey—the one that ends in adulthood. For many, this involves leaving home, family and friends for a new and rather foreign environment and lifestyle. He's headed to Texas A&M, and we can safely bet that his world will never be quite the same. It will be better in many ways, and worse in others, but it will inevitably be there, and he will be in it.

Each of your parents can relate to this life transition, because we've all been through it. As we watch you go, we remember the mix of excitement, anxiety, freedom, daring and responsibility that will never quite exist in the same balance again. Only a few weeks ago, I found myself in Western Kansas reliving the moment in August 1981 when I saw my hometown disappear in my review mirror. Twenty-six years later, it is one of the most powerful memories of my life. Each of us has one. As graduating seniors, you're about to make yours.

Your parents are living this week on the other side of goodbye, a different but no less important experience. It's the moment when they find themselves reflected in *your* review mirror, reminded of the remarkably short time they serve as parents of children, before moving on to their far longer and even more joyful role as parents of adults.

In some areas, you might have a deuce; in others, a Queen. But all of us, if we look hard enough, have four aces in that deck.

John has been a great colleague this year and I've enjoyed watching him develop his writing. His closing column today is a fine example of his remarkable way with words. Each of us is really the sum of everyone who's influenced, loved and cared for us along the way. I hope that somewhere down the road, we'll see a little bit of Double Take in John, just as each of our readers take with them a little bit of him.

John Murray: I started writing this column under the impression that I would teach readers the finer points of life. But the more I wrote, the more I realized that *it* was teaching *me*. It taught me the challenges of consistently writing a regular piece and to appreciate the journalists who do it every day. It encouraged me to work creatively even when I did not have immediate inspiration. It reminded me never to judge another person by what I can see on the outside, because we all have secrets in our daily lives.

The high school experience can be terrifying, so I'd like to close by passing on two pieces of advice I wish I'd heard more often.

First, if you can handle each week as it comes, the years will fall into place. I spent many high school nights wondering where I was going to be in four years when I should have been reviewing what I had to do tomorrow.

Second, don't worry about what you will become. You were born with a deck of cards containing all your talents and natural abilities. In some areas, you might have a deuce; in others, a Queen. But all of us, if we look hard enough, have four aces in that deck.

The primary goal of your young adult life is to find those four aces. You'll have plenty of time to develop your talents in adulthood, but for now, just look for your niche. Don't be afraid to change your career outlook several times, or to pick a vocation others didn't expect of you. Just find the career that's right for you, and put your best efforts behind it.

To paraphrase Martin Luther King Jr., "There's no shame in being a street-sweeper, if you sweep streets like Michelangelo painted pictures and Beethoven composed music."

Weird Places

Dr. Wes: This week we conclude Julia Davidson's year on Double Take. While all the co-authors to date have been seniors, Julia took the reigns as a rising junior. To be honest, I had some apprehension about this. Could a junior find her voice while still shy of the top of the high school pyramid? Had she been through enough hazing at sixteen to deal with some of the less seemly postings that come from anonymous access to the blogosphere? What about follow-through and responsibility? The deadlines are fierce, and if either of us gets off track or behind during the week, the other has to flex to pull things back together.

I had nothing to worry about.

Julia has been a joy to work with. She's put her thoughts out there in a humorous and honest style, made her deadlines, flexed as needed, brushed off meaningless critique, and taken to heart that which is well-intentioned.

As a therapist, I work to liberate kids from troubling circumstances, whether self-imposed, put upon them by others, psychological or social. In Double Take, we bring that dialog into the public eye, so perhaps we can find out how much we're all alike as well as how to handle the many differences we face, together. In a column designed to address the struggles, fears, issues and shortcomings of teenagers and their parents, Julia has been a celebration of what's right with kids today.

Julia Davidson: I am in a weird place, writing my final column, literally and figuratively. I am in Berlin, typing away while my friends and family are asleep. But I'm also in a weird place because of the exact time in my life I find myself writing a reflective piece. As Wes said, only seniors have written for Double Take before, meaning only *seniors* have completed a final column bursting at the seams with senior-derived wisdom. They're in a prime spot for looking back on the nostalgia of their high school days and ahead to their newfound young-adulthood.

The truth is I am, like all rising seniors, scared. Yet I remain unrelenting in trying to make it look easy, which it is not.

I am not one of them. For one more week, I am a junior, and reflecting on junior year is like trying to find beauty in a very bad smell...or in putting your hand through a meat grinder. Pre-reflecting on senior year makes me shudder with anticipation and apprehension. I'm baby steps away from becoming a legal adult, but already starting to be considered one.

"Where are you going to college?" plays in my head like an irritating jingle as mail floods in from every university on earth and ACTs and SATs weigh on my mind. Beyond the academic perspective, independence and responsibility sit on my shoulders like an angel and a devil. All too soon decisions will be tougher and my friendships and relationships will be tested. I don't know if I'm old enough to be in love, move away, or live alone, and at times, I feel much too young to be flung into this high-speed adult world.

To top it off, I don't know where to look for answers. I can look back and glean nuggets from past school experiences or look ahead and wonder about an unknown final school year. Today, I find myself sitting between both perspectives, dizzy as all get out.

The truth is I am, like all rising seniors, scared—I'm scared from junior year and scared for senior year—but yet I remain unrelenting in trying to make it look easy, which it is not. The end of senior year isn't the only time for mixed and extreme emotions. Even now, we are required to make permanent decisions by ourselves, testing our maturity and sense of self. It is simultaneously exciting, difficult and thrilling.

Yes, I'm in a very weird place.

But often those places produce the best results. Being in a weird place takes you out of your comfort zone and forces you to adapt. You learn what you believe—without other factors influencing your opinion—as you question your surroundings. Weird places test and prove who you really are, and luckily, as I move along in my personal journey, I've been able to share my experience with many other people.

Ciao...or shall I say "auf weidershein" everyone!

Reinventing Yourself

Dr. Wes: As the heat of August peaks, we look ahead to fall, the pause before a cold leafless winter, a last time for festivals and picnics, yard work and home improvement; football, volleyball and homecoming. Teens feel recharged for a moment, ready to face the challenges ahead, of which there will be many.

For recent graduates, a distance will open in the coming weeks between you and your folks, which will only continue to grow. The unsteady freshman and sophomore years at college, or the struggles of a new entry-level job. There will be a change of plan or two. A reversal of fortune—dropping out of school or going for the first time. Then a stabilizing, for some sooner than others. Another graduation, a degree or trade. A family. Or, for so many clients I see now, early divorce.

For most in their mid-twenties, there will come a renewal of family ties—especially if parents have made that relationship strong in your teen years and reinforced it with a balance of boundaries and support in young adulthood.

Almost thirty years ago, when my own father faced the August of my departure, friends asked whether he wasn't sad to see his only child driving three hundred miles to college in an antique pickup truck. We weren't wealthy, so trips home would be rare, yet my father offered those folks the same advice I will offer your parents now. He said, "I'm not sad at all. That's the whole purpose of being a parent."

Readers of Double Take experience another loss each August, as we transition from one teen co-author to the next. This marks the fiftieth and final column written by Samantha Schwartz, who leaves us shortly for Grinnell College in Iowa. It's hard for me to adequately sum up how I feel about losing Sam. Perhaps the best measure of her value to this column is the number of times over the year that I've been approached by readers

Moving is the self-guided trail to the rest of my life, not the edge of a cliff. I've learned to embrace change rather than fear it.

who describe her work on Double Take with words like "outstanding," "really good advice," and "so insightful." All this lopsided praise would make me feel terribly insecure in her shadow if I didn't wholeheartedly agree with it. Working with her has challenged me to write better, think harder and, at times, just give up and follow her lead. Exactly what I'm looking for in a co-author—a partner and colleague.

So, I'll feel her loss deeply, as will our readers.

It is often said that good things must come to an end, with little explanation as to why. Without ends, there can be no beginnings. Teenagers must leave home to become adults. Double Take must say goodbye to take the next step forward.

Each year I ask the outgoing writer to give us what amounts to her commencement speech, a chance to freelance her views on this time of transition. Not surprisingly, Sam's final column closes out her tenure in style.

Samantha Schwartz: When I was thirteen, I would have rather lost my pinky finger than have been forced to move away from my California hometown. At that time, change was terrifying. When I heard we were moving, I immediately began to mourn the loss of my friends, my school and my house. In typical thirteen-year-old fashion, I made a PowerPoint presentation ornamented with clipart trashcans entitled, "WHY ARE YOU THROWING AWAY MY LIFE?"

I made myself miserable for months anticipating that I wouldn't be happy in any other place. Instead of enjoying the limited time I had with friends and family in California, I grieved over leaving until I left. A few months later, in my new hometown, I was happier than I'd ever been.

Moving allowed me to reinvent myself and become the person I had always wanted to be.

Now, as an eighteen-year-old, moving is exhilarating. Everything will be different, and that's a good thing. Moving is the self-guided trail to the rest of my life, not the edge of a cliff.

I've learned to embrace change rather than fear it. You'd be surprised what kind of advantage that gives you in the world. It's like buying lottery tickets; the more changes you let into your life, the more chances you have to succeed. Life will change whether or not you're a willing participant. Take it from the Greek philosopher Heraclitus: change is the only constant.

Present Tense

Dr. Wes: Each year in August our new author is asked to pick any topic he or she wishes to write about for the first column. If this represents a sample of Ben's typical work, I'd say we're in for a great year.

Ben Markley: This year has proved to be one of new experiences for me. Not only am I taking this new position as a co-author of Double Take, but I also hiked my first mountain with some buddies over the summer. At the beginning, I remember being completely taken with the beautiful Colorado scenery. The view from the side of the mountain was nothing short of majestic. I was so glad to be right where I was.

Pause for a second. Breathe. Take a look around. You'll get to the summit eventually.

Then, I hiked up a few thousand feet. Being a writer and not an athlete, I was exhausted, and toward the end of our hike, I couldn't care less about the scenery. My two primary thoughts were the summit at the top of the mountain and the pickup truck at the bottom. I didn't care where I was. All I could think about was where I wasn't.

I had a similar experience writing my first column. I was excited by the chance to give our readers my two cents. As I struggled for a topic, however, my mind got ahead of itself. Could I really produce a year's worth of columns? What problems would readers throw at me? What if I really didn't have an answer?

After about half an hour of speculation, I was still staring at a blank screen.

As teenagers, we're often accused of living as if there were no consequences—we're so in the moment that we ignore our future. That is true for a lot of teens, and sometimes we need a reminder. Others try to live only in the future, and still others are stuck in the past. We dwell anywhere but the present.

I'm well acquainted with high school seniors who are freaking out over where they're going to college or what their major will be. I've also met my share of sophomores who just can't stop talking about their middle school memories. They're looking in two different directions, but they're both ignoring one very important thing—today.

Surely, we should remember the past and consider the future, but only as they inform what we do in the present. Each is a means to an end, not an end in and of itself. People who live in yesterday become obsessed with nostalgia, while those who live in tomorrow become romantic procrastinators.

So, pause for a second. Breathe. Take a look around. You'll get to the summit eventually.

Until then, enjoy the scenery.

Snow Day Couple Reprise

Dear Dr. Wes and Miranda,

On March 9th, 2010 you wrote a Double Take column about meeting a couple at Chili's[12]. That article was about my boyfriend and me. I wanted to write and just thank you for being such a kind stranger and for writing about Daniel and me. I cut out the article the day I found it and put it on my wall, but Daniel (being the man he is) read it once and forgot about it.

Well, in August, Daniel shipped off to West Point for military training and has been homesick off and on. On a day he was feeling pretty bad, I mailed him that article. When he got it, he called me up and thanked me, admitting that seeing it again made him tear up a little bit.

---

[12] The "Snow Day Couple" column opens Chapter 2 of this book. I received Taylor's email just before Christmas in 2011 and we ran it the following week. We decided to open and close this book with their story because it illustrates what Double Take has always been about—helping young people find the best future possible by making the best choices possible. In a world filled with millions of bad options for teens, Taylor and Daniel are my heroes. They're picking the good ones.

Thank you for giving me the opportunity to bring a little light into his world. You didn't have to approach us that snow day and tell us that you thought we were cute. You didn't even have to write that article. But you did. I'll put that column on display at our wedding and it will be something we'll show our kids. (Don't worry. We're not jumping the gun or anything :p).

We're forever grateful.

—Taylor

Dr. Wes: Over the years, I've had many joys writing Double Take, but none greater than receiving your letter. A few months after that column ran, I tried telling your story to one of my clients—a teenage girl. I only got as far as mentioning "the couple at Chili's" before she stopped me and said, "I read that column, Wes. I know their story. Everybody does. It's on everyone's Facebook." A few months after that, another girl told me that she'd figured out who you were and had actually contacted you. She told me you were still together, which brightened my day.

It is a wonderful treat to hear how your story continues now; how you've found a way to keep your love alive, even as Daniel is far away serving his country. You've lost your boy to West Point, which puts you among an elite group of young women throughout history who have bravely given up the daily touch and loving comfort of a young man and have released him to a higher calling of honor and service. Each of you has sacrificed the luxury of the present moment in order to build a brighter future together, and there is no greater sign of love than that.

This couple demonstrates to everyone how a relationship should be, which is way more effective than any advice we could give.

Our advice in this column is that long distance relationships at your age rarely survive. No one can know whether yours will be the exception, but as Samantha Schwartz and I observed almost two years ago, the foundation you've built gives you an unusually good chance. Have courage. Be patient. Let Daniel know how much you miss him and, just as often, how much you support him. Take every chance you can to be with him, and when you can't, use technology to your advantage. Above all else, whenever he falters, say the words that matter most: "I believe in you, and the 'us' we're creating together."

I'd wish you luck, Taylor, but you won't need it. You have each other.

Miranda Davis: As people who know me will tell you, I'm not a romantic girl. Sometimes I feel as though I'm missing my own "teenage girl" mindset. Even so, when I originally read Samantha and Wes's column about the "Snow Day" couple, I was touched. These two seemed to defy the odds, as if having a real, functional relationship in high school was the easiest thing in the world. For those who haven't tried it yet, someday you'll understand how truly remarkable their accomplishment is.

What Sam said two years ago still resonates with me: Taylor and Daniel's relationship is no accident. From her recent letter I've gathered that their hard work has only gotten harder. Not only has their love survived high school, but also college, the real world, the military, and a half-a-continent of distance. They've given their relationship about a hundred more odds to defy, and they're still doing a good job.

We can tell you over and over again not to date a "bad boy," or to not let someone toss around your emotions. But this couple demonstrates to everyone who has heard their story how a relationship should be, which is way more effective than any advice we could give.

I hope our readers see their story not as a fairytale but as real life—what each of us could have if we put in that kind of effort and devotion. Teens have this idea that a relationship should be easy and simple. Instead, think about this couple and their daily struggles to be together, apart.

It's a pretty incredible feeling knowing that this column can bring people happiness, not just advice. Though I was not part of the original story, it warms my heart that Double Take meant so much to Taylor and that it helped eased Daniel's homesickness. I wish these two a lifetime of loving, happy dates, wearing sweatpants in a booth at Chili's, and sharing kisses across the table.

Maybe they'll keep writing in and telling us how they're doing.

ABOUT THE AUTHORS

Wes Crenshaw, PhD is a licensed psychologist and Board Certified in Couples and Family Psychology by the American Board of Professional Psychology. He specializes in working with adolescents and their families from his private practice in Lawrence, KS. He is the author of *Treating Families and Children in the Child Protective System* (Brunner-Routledge, 2004) and chapters several in other textbooks. He has co-authored Double Take since November 2004. Dr. Wes has been married since 1985 (to the same woman, no less) and has two children, including a teenager who helped him immensely in both the conceptualization and final editing of this book. He is presently working on another set of books based on Double Take, while finishing his novels. You can learn more about his writing and practice and submit your own question to Double Take at www.dr-wes.com or follow his advice for parents and teens on Twitter at @wescrenshawphd.

Jenny Kane (2004-2005) discovered her passion for journalism working on Double Take. After graduation from Free State High School she went to Western Kentucky University to pursue her dream of becoming a photojournalist. While in school she interned for the Topeka Capitol-Journal, The Oregonian, and the Monroe Evening News. In 2010 she graduated with degrees in Photojournalism (emphasis in multi-media) and Political Science. After graduation she spent a year at the Patriot-News as a post-graduate fellow. Currently, she is working for the Northwest Herald in Crystal Lake, Il as a video journalist. Follow her work at www.jennykane.com.

Marissa Ballard Hemenway (Co-author, 2005-2006) graduated with a BS in Education from Pittsburg State University. She married her junior high sweetheart, Arna Hemenway, in July of 2010 as described at the end of Chapter 2 in this book. In October of 2011, they welcomed a daughter, Bluma, making Marissa the first Double Take author to start her own countdown to parenting an adolescent. The Hemenways are currently living in Iowa, where we will forward future editions of these books in exactly thirteen years.

John Murray (Co-author, 2006-2007) recently received his B.A. in Philosophy from the University of Kansas. He enjoys reading about rational choice theory and playing Settlers of Catan, hopefully in moderation as he recommends in his column in Chapter 8 of *Dear Dr. Wes: Real Life Advice for Teens*. His current projects include learning Python programming and teaching his little brother economics.

Julia Davidson (Co-author, 2007-2008) is a second-semester junior at Macalester College in St. Paul, Minnesota. She is currently working on a combined major in Theater and Dance with a Critical Theory concentration. In her free time, she goes on long walks and coffee dates with her friends. Julia's future hopes and dreams include working in the field of dance and bodywork, incorporating the caring and compassion rooted in the realm of therapy. Her present hopes and dreams are for the success of this book, the continuation of the Double Take column, and the best cup of coffee in town!

Kelly Kelin Woods (Co-author, 2008-2009) is an undergraduate at the University of Kansas. She is currently majoring in English and hopes one day to become a writer. After graduation she plans on traveling around the world to look for potential graduate school opportunities to further her career and life experience.

Samantha Schwartz (Co-author, 2009-2010) is a sophomore at Grinnell College in Iowa, majoring in psychology. If you've read her advice in this book, you'll know why. In fact, she currently works as a Wellness Coordinator at her college, working to make a difference in both the physical and mental health of other students. She plans to attend graduate school in 2014 to pursue a PhD in psychology, and hopes to focus once again on teen issues—about which she has proven her expertise time and again in the pages of this book (photo by *Insight Photography*, Lawrence, KS).

Ben Markley (Co-author, 2010-2011) graduated from Lawrence Free State High School in 2011 and is currently attending Johnson County Community College where he is studying creative writing and philosophy. He is considering seminary after he earns a bachelor's degree and hopes to pursue a writing career in the future. That won't surprise Double Take readers, given the number of comments we received during his year on both the quality and style of his work.

Miranda Davis (Co-author, 2011-present) is a senior at Lawrence Free State High School and co-editor-in-chief of the *Free State Free Press*. She admits that, as a freshman, she read Samantha Schwartz's advice every week and considered her "the most brilliant teenager ever." That apparently paid off, because three years later Miranda won her chance to be brilliant. After graduating in May, she plans to attend the University of Kansas to study journalism. Miranda showed special courage in serving her term on Double Take at the same time this book was being complied and sent to press, allowing her to put up with more than her share of "Dr. Wes Stress."

About Our Town

Lawrence, Kansas was burned and sacked and its citizens murdered before it was ten years old. Twice. Not surprisingly, its symbol is The Phoenix. Certain folks in Missouri didn't agree with our liberal views on slavery back in the 1850s and 60s, and we still have border clashes with them to this day. Fortunately those take place on the basketball and football fields now. In honor of our history one of our high schools, a credit union, and a famous brewery now go by the name Free State as an homage to that radical notion of freedom for all.

Lawrence remains a unique, progressive, and vibrant intellectual and artistic community. It is home to the University of Kansas, a school of

29,000 undergraduate and graduate students, and Haskell Indian Nations University, a four-year college of 1000 students from Native American tribes all over the United States.

Having lived here now for twenty-three years, Dr. Wes is convinced that few other towns would have embraced Double Take as has Lawrence. We are still a community that believes in doing things a little differently than everyone else, and we do so proudly.